D1243443

THE WILD WEST

Plate I. Peaux Rouges By Pierre Bonnard

The inspiration for this painting came from the Wild West show,
probably Buffalo Bill's Wild West, which toured Europe in 1889, or
Pawnee Bill's Historic Wild West, which visited Belgium, Holland and
France in 1894-1895.

Oil on panel. 9 x 11 inches. ca. 1895.

Amon Carter Museum Collection.

The Amon Carter Museum was established in 1961 under the will of the late Amon G. Carter for the study and documentation of westering North America. The program of the Museum, expressed in publications, exhibitions, and permanent collections, reflects many aspects of American culture, both historic and contemporary.

Introduction

MAIN
c. 1

An exhibition-publication project on the origins, etc., of the **Wild West Show** has been on the museum agenda for an unduly long time. Our first efforts were confounded by trying to accomplish too much; an examination of early day traveling shows and circuses in the West; "Mud Shows," rodeos, *jaripeos, corridas,* and Indian pow-pows. Leonard Farley, then curator of the Hertzberg Circus Collection of the San Antonio Public Library, pointed out the error of our ways, indicating the need to dissect the problem. Rebecca Salsbury James, daughter of Cody's business colleague, Nate Salsbury, focused our efforts through her hilarious firsthand accounts of life in the home of a Wild West entrepreneur. It is much to my regret that Becky James did not live to share our fun in putting the show together.

Finally, Barbara Tyler, until recently curator of history in the Carter Museum, took the project to Don Russell, the acknowledged founthead of Buffalo Bill wisdom. It is a pity we didn't find him earlier, but our record of indecision and delays is all the more credible when contrasted with Mr. Russell's enthusiasm and savvy on all matters western. He has led us out of the wilderness.

Dr. Ronnie C. Tyler of the museum staff has edited the publication and organized the materials of our exhibition. Our debt to collectors, libraries, and other museums is acknowledged elsewhere.

Mitchell A. Wilder

Fort Worth
January 29, 1970

Contents

Color Plates

FIRST EPISODE—
A Dazzling Prelude to a Mighty Spectacle

Buffalo Bill, sometimes known more formally as William Frederick Cody, but not yet dubbed Colonel, came home to North Platte, Nebraska, in the early summer of 1882, at the close of his tenth season in stage melodrama. As the late William McDonald, who was there at the time, later told me, Cody came into Charles J. Foley's store. Charles F. Ormsby, onetime mayor of North Platte, and other leading citizens were already there. Cody asked what had been planned for celebrating the Fourth of July. When he was told that nothing had been planned, McDonald remembered that "Cody mumbled something to the effect that he was surprised that nothing had been planned for the Fourth of July, then he went up the street to the saloon, but he hardly stayed long enough to get a drink. He wasn't one to take a drink just to get his mouth wet. He came back, protesting that it was not patriotic not to have a Fourth of July celebration. Ormsby and Foley said, 'O. K., Bill, you are chairman to get up a celebration.' "[1]

Independence Day has had its periods of neglect since 1882, so Cody's sense of outrage may not be fully appreciated. Since 1776 the celebration of the Fourth of July had been *the* national holiday. Not only did towns and cities throughout the country plan celebrations, but Western explorers, wagon trains and travelers on the Santa Fe and other trails halted in their tracks on July 4, to celebrate the day in some way. Even the need to keep moving so as to avoid being caught by disastrous snows as was the Donner party, did not keep them from stopping to fire off guns, drink up what liquor was left, and hold a jubilation. Independence Rock in Wyoming marks the site of one of these Oregon Trail holidays.

So Buffalo Bill set about planning North Platte's "Old Glory Blow Out." There are those who have doubted his energy and his managerial ability, but he manifested both this time. The arena was a race track with a fence around it. Buffalo Bill proposed to give a

---

[1] Don Russell, *The Lives and Legends of Buffalo Bill* (Norman: University of Oklahoma Press, 1960), pp. 290-291.

demonstration of his methods of killing buffalo, using steers and blank ammunition. McDonald recalled that M. C. Keefe had a small herd of buffalo that might be borrowed. Cody persuaded business men to offer prizes for roping, shooting, riding, and bronco breaking events and 5,000 handbills were sent out. Cody estimated he might get 100 cowboy entrants; he actually got 1,000. It has been said that no similar event ever had so many able competitors. The unprecedented and unexpected success gave Cody an idea. McDonald later said that Buffalo Bill, at that time, announced his intention of organizing a Wild West show, using that name for it.

That Fourth of July, 1882, in North Platte marks the beginnings of both the Wild West show and the rodeo. It was not, probably, the "first" for either. Historians, especially historians of the local and the specific, overstress priority. No city or county history fails to give full detail on the first settler, with rarely a suggestion that if there had not been a second settler, and third settler, and a great many more settlers, no city would ever have been incorporated or no county organized.

Neither is it necessary to go back to the horsemen of Crete, Troy, or Mycenae to find predecessors for the acts programmed by Buffalo Bill's Wild West as "Cowboy Fun." Rodeo historians are sound in tracing their sport to the by-play and show-off of early cattle round-ups. Captain Mayne Reid, author of *The Scalp Hunters* and *The Rifle Rangers*, wrote from Santa Fe in 1847: "This round-up is a great time for the cowhands, a Donnybrook fair it is indeed. They contest with each other for the best roping and throwing, and there are horse races and whiskey and wines."[2]

The Wild West was brought to New York as early as 1843, by way of Boston, where a herd of yearling buffalo had been exhibited at the celebration dedicating Bunker Hill monument. P. T. Barnum bought the herd and announced a one-day "Grand Buffalo Hunt," free to the public in Hoboken — after he had chartered the ferry-boats for the day. His hunter roped a calf or two, and a free band concert helped the crowd enjoy being humbugged, according to Barnum.[3]

Tyler's Indian Exhibition also put on a buffalo hunt, as well as

---

[2]Quoted in Clifford P. Westermeier, *Trailing the Cowboy* (Caldwell, Idaho: Caxton Printers, 1955), pp. 343-344.

[3]P. T. Barnum, *Struggles and Triumphs* (New York: Macmillan Company, 1930), pp. 94-95.

dances, a corn festival, and a spectacle of Pocahontas rescuing Captain John Smith. It toured in 1855 with Van Amburgh's menagerie and Den Stone's circus, and in 1856 with Mabie Brothers menagerie and Den Stone. This was the period in which various types of shows were combining in a trend toward the American three-ring circus. Isaac A. Van Amburgh became the "Lion King" in 1820 and organized his menagerie the following year. His name survived in circus billing as late as 1908. Ed F. and Jerry Mabie were independent operators from 1840 to 1864. They pioneered in night shows and in the after-show minstrels.[4]

James Capen Adams, known as Grizzly Adams, assembled his menagerie by hunting, trapping, and training his animals in California. In 1860 he took his menagerie by ship around the Horn to New York where he made a deal with P. T. Barnum. The parade opening the California Menagerie is described by Barnum:

> A band of music preceded a procession of animal cages down Broadway and up the Bowery, Old Adams dressed in his hunting costume, heading the line with a platform wagon on which were placed three immense grizzly bears, two of which he held by chains, while he was mounted on the back of the largest grizzly, which stood in the centre and was not secured in any manner whatever. This was the bear known as "General Frémont," and so docile had he become that Adams said he had used him as a pack-bear to carry his cooking and hunting apparatus through the mountains for six months, and had ridden him hundreds of miles.[5]

The Wild West was never wilder than this.

Getting back to "Cowboy Fun," Emilne Gardenshire of the Milliron Ranch was declared "champion bronco buster of the plains" at a Fourth of July celebration in 1869 at Deer Trail, Colorado. The riding of a wild steer was a Fourth of July event in Cheyenne in 1872. In that same year, August 28 and 30, Wild Bill Hickok had a brief fling at the Grand Buffalo Hunt. This affair was staged by Sidney Barnett at Niagara Falls. A newspaper account says only three buffalo were present and "several" Indians and Mexicans, and that "the skill of these men in riding and lassoing is remarkable." Cayuga and Tuscarora Indians, living nearby, played lacrosse. That is the extent of Wild Bill's contribution to the Wild West show. He is said to have made an appearance in Colonel Ginger's circus at

[4]Elbert R. Bowen, "The Circus in Early Rural Missouri," *Missouri Historical Review*, XLVII (October, 1952), 12; George L. Chindahl, *A History of the Circus in America* (Caldwell, Idaho: Caxton Printers, 1959), pp. 268-269.
[5]Barnum, *Struggles and Triumphs*, pp. 383-384; Tracy I. Storer and Lloyd P. Tevis, Jr., *California Grizzly* (Berkeley: University of California Press, 1955), pp. 217-238.

Dr. W. F. Carver, "Evil Spirit of the Plains" and champion rifle shot, was Buffalo Bill's first partner, toured Europe and Australia with his own show, and ended his long showman's career with a diving horse act.
Amon Carter Museum Collection.

Nate Salsbury, long-time partner of Buffalo Bill and originator of its Congress of Rough Riders of the World feature.
Amon Carter Museum Collection.

Pawnee Bill (Gordon W. Lillie) headed his own Pawnee Bill Historic Wild West and Great Far East show, merged in 1908 with Buffalo Bill's Wild West.
Courtesy of Western History Collections, University of Oklahoma Library.

Iron Tail, one of a very few Indians featured in posters, headed the Indians on Buffalo Bill's Wild West for many years, and later appeared in the Miller Bros. 101 Ranch show. He was advertised as the Indian on the buffalo nickle.
Gertrude Käsebier, photographer; Courtesy of the Library of Congress.

Sherman, Texas. He toured in stage melodrama for part of one season with Buffalo Bill, and more briefly on his own. He was married in 1876 to Mrs. Agnes Lake, who owned a circus, but he was killed in Deadwood that year, and made no show appearances with her.[6]

Thus we see that many of the elements that made up Buffalo Bill's Wild West were already in existence when William F. Cody got his idea for a new type of outdoor entertainment. What was new about it was their combination in a formula that spelled success. And success is the criterion that nullifies others' claims, including two of his sometime partners, that they originated the Wild West idea.

A few definitions may clear the air at this point. The word "circus" was always anathema on the Buffalo Bill lot. So was "show." The billing was invariably "Buffalo Bill's Wild West" without the added explanatory "show." If cornered on this, its general manager and press agent, John M. Burke, certainly one of the world's top publicists, would insist that it was an exhibition. Arizona John's ban on "show" is unrealistic and will not be followed "out the window" in these pages. Therefore a Wild West show may be defined as an exhibition illustrating scenes and events characteristic of the American Far West frontier — and that definition is cribbed in part from Arizona John Burke himself.[7]

Rodeo is derived in part from the Wild West show, but from only one part. Rodeo is a competitive sport in which the contestants pay an entrance fee and receive no pay except from prize money. Rodeos are produced locally under standards approved by the Rodeo Cowboys Association. A traveling rodeo of hired contestants would fit the definition of a Wild West show.

The circus is an older form of outdoor entertainment. Two histories have been named *The Circus from Rome to Ringling*,[8] but neither makes a successful connection with Rome's *circus maximus*. The circus probably came closest to Rome in the late nineteenth century when, inspired by the popularity of General Lew Wallace's novel *Ben-Hur*, it introduced the Roman chariot race on the hippodrome

[6]Joseph G. Rosa, *They Called Him Wild Bill* (Norman: University of Oklahoma Press, 1964), pp. 112-116.

[7]*Buffalo Bill's Wild West and Congress of Rough Riders of the World. Historical Sketches and Programme* (Chicago: Blakely Printing Company, 1893), p. 4.

[8]Earl Chapin May, *The Circus from Rome to Ringling* (New York: Duffield and Green, 1932); Marion Murray, *Circus: From Rome to Ringling* (New York: Appleton, 1956).

track. As the novel had won approval for its religious content, this exhibition helped to relieve the prejudice of many sectarians against such frivolous entertainment as the circus.

While the circus derived little from Rome except the name, it has a more direct link with the traveling performers who followed the medieval trade fairs. Another form of outdoor entertainment, the carnival, still plays fairs. The recognized progenitor, however, was Philip Astley who opened in 1770 a one-ring circus in London, featuring horsemanship acts. The European circus stayed close to Astley's one-ring presentation, often in a fixed location, although adding clowns, acrobats, jugglers, trapeze artists, trained animals, and other acts that now seem part and parcel of all circuses.

In America the trend was toward size and movement. The circus as a horse show arrived almost immediately. A Mr. Faulks was performing feats of horsemanship in Philadelphia in 1771. More famous was John Bill Ricketts who toured from 1792 to 1799 and was seen by George Washington. Ricketts also anticipated the Wild West show; one of his "specs" was based on the Whiskey Rebellion in western Pennsylvania.

Thus the spectacle, if not the show world's jargon for it, "spec," goes back to circus beginnings in America. It started with the walk-around, or parade, of all performers at the beginning of the show, but might be elaborated into "Julius Caesar, A Picturesque Revival of the Sports of Ancient Rome," or a reproduction of Villa's attack on Columbus, New Mexico, the same year that it happened — both of which were spectacles of the 101 Ranch Wild West Show.

Even earlier on the American scene was the traveling menagerie, showing strange creatures to people who had no other opportunity to view them. When Hachaliah Bailey imported an elephant in 1808 the American circus was on its way. It became an amalgamation of the horse show, menagerie, the trained animal show, the museum of freaks, and the hippodrome track for races that proved so useful in staging the Ben-Hur chariot race. The hippodrome track enclosed a large area, necessitating three rings, eventually separated by two stages, a set-up that became standard for any circus daring to call itself "the greatest show on earth."

Horses not only were the top performers; they also were the motive power to move the show from place to place. Wagons creaked along through the night, halting at the edge of town to make triumphal entry for awakening citizens. Thus developed the circus parade, eventually featuring specially-made wagons, elaborately decorated with wood carvings, among them a band wagon to lead the procession and a calliope to give it a loud and raucous conclusion.

Circuses took to the railroads as fast as useful trackage was available. Longer jumps to larger cities brought larger profits — and bigger circuses. Den Stone was a pioneer on the rails in 1854 and Spalding & Rogers Railroad Circus was billed in 1856. Dan Castello's Circus and Menagerie played Savannah, Georgia, on the Atlantic coast in February, 1869, which may be remembered as the year the golden spike was driven to complete the first transcontinental railroad. By the time that spike joined the Union Pacific and the Central Pacific railroads, Dan Castello's show was far enough west to go on through and it finished its season on the Pacific coast. Circumstantial evidence indicates that Buffalo Bill saw that show at North Platte in the interval between two Indian expeditions he accompanied as scout from nearby Fort McPherson. W. C. Coup, as partner of P. T. Barnum, is credited with designing the system for unloading special circus trains by using a continuous ramp in 1871.

Circuses reached the Pacific coast long before Dan Castello got there on the first transcontinental railroad. Joseph Andrew Rowe was touring South America when he heard about the California Gold Rush. He lost no time in shipping out of Peru. Rowe's Olympic Circus opened in San Francisco October 29, 1849. He came back in 1856 with a new name. It was now Rowe & Co.'s Pioneer Circus.[9] These examples indicate how closely show business followed the frontier.

In the present century, when live entertainment is a luxury, it is not easy to understand how these huge and expensive aggregations could make a profit from small audiences at fifty cents for one ticket that admitted the holder to all events. Of course many of them failed to make it. Outdoor show business was a precarious occupation. Buffalo Bill's Wild West was launched on the upswing in 1883. That was not entirely fortuitous; Cody had behind him a decade of successful stage melodrama. It was the beginning of the Golden Age of the Circus. By 1885 fifty and more shows were on the road, the top number at any time. There were such familiar names as P. T. Barnum, James A. Bailey, Adam Forepaugh, Sells Brothers, John Robinson, W. W. Cole, with Ben Wallace and Ringling Brothers just

[9]Chang Reynolds, *Pioneer Circuses of the West* (Los Angeles: Westernlore Press, 1966), pp. 14-30.

getting started. The period of merger and consolidation came later: Barnum & Bailey; Forepaugh & Sells Brothers, Wallace & Hagenbeck.

Cody continued his theatrical season through the winter of 1882-1883, but he also signed up talent and sought properties for the show he was planning. Nate Salsbury had proposed a partnership with Cody, but Nate was not ready that winter. Nate afterward claimed that he had originated the Wild West. A discussion of the merits of Australian, Mexican, and American cowboy riding had given him the idea. "I began to construct a show in my mind that would embody the whole subject of horsemanship," he says, "a show that would be constituted of elements that had never been employed in concerted effort in the history of show business." This concept suggests the "Congress of Rough Riders of the World" feature that did not become part of the show until 1891 with no hint of the pageant of the West that Cody had in mind.[10]

During his tour Cody met Dr. William F. Carver in New Haven and the result was a partnership. Carver also claimed to be the originator of the Wild West idea, although curiously the first quarrel of the partners was over Cody's use of "Wild West" in billing printed instead of the "Golden West" that Carver preferred.[11]

Carver billed himself as "Champion Shot of the World" and as he had toured Europe from 1879 to 1882 challenging all comers, the claim had some validity. His scores of record were in endurance contests. In 1888 in Minneapolis he hit 60,000 wooden blocks tossed in air with only 650 misses, a six-day job. The next year B. A. Bartlett of Buffalo made the 60,000 with only 280 misses and in 1907 Adolph T. Topperwein, the all-time expert at this sort of thing, hit 72,500 targets with only nine misses. Still Doc Carver had a good reputation as

[10]Nate Salsbury, "The Origin of the Wild West Show," *Colorado Magazine*, XXXII (July, 1955), 204-214.

[11]Raymond W. Thorp, *Spirit Gun of the West; The Story of Doc W. F. Carver* (Glendale: Arthur H. Clark Company, 1957), p. 138. See also articles by Thorp: "Doc Carver vs. Buffalo Bill," *Real West*, X (March-May, 1967), 18-20, 30-34, 53, 72-73; "He Challenged the Champions," *Guns*, V (June, 1959), 14-16, 46-49; "The Letters of Doc Carver," *Outdoor Life — Outdoor Recreation*, LXV, LXVI (April-July, 1930), 18-21, 18-20, 30-31, 50-52, 88-89, 100; also see the *Western Horseman*, February-April, 1940. Less laudatory are E. L. Stevenson, "Those Carver Yarns," *Outdoor Life — Outdoor Recreation*, LXVI (August, 1930), 22-23, 82-84; and Charles B. Roth, "The Biggest Blow Since Galveston," *Denver Westerners Monthly Roundup*, XII (January, 1956), 1, 5-14. For additional facts on Carver's early life I am indebted to Paul D. Riley, research associate, Nebraska State Historical Society.

Parades were the most lavish and expensive publicity
devices of circuses and Wild West shows. Buffalo Bill (above), in full costume,
leads his troupe through downtown Denver. The horsedrawn parade wagon
(with the longhorn on top) attracted attention in the 101 Ranch Wild West Show parade.
Courtesy of the State Historical Society of Colorado and the
Western History Collections, University of Oklahoma Library.

marksman. He also billed himself as "Evil Spirit of the Plains," which he claimed had been conferred upon him by Spotted Tail of the Brulé Sioux. His "daring exploits on the frontier" depend almost entirely upon his own yarns recorded in interviews during his shooting tours, and in these he often failed to agree with himself.

A few facts about him have come to light. William Frank Carver was born May 7, 1851, at Winslow, Illinois, the son of William Daniel Carver, a practicing physician, and Deborah Tohapenes (Peters) Carver. They had two other children, William Pitt who became a farmer in Kansas and May who died in infancy. The parents came to Illinois from Pennsylvania in 1849. Not much more is known about Doc Carver until he arrived at Fort McPherson, Nebraska, in August, 1872. He practiced dentistry there and in North Platte. He filed on a homestead claim on Medicine Creek north of Stockville, Frontier County, and was joined there by his mother and brother in 1874. Carver passed much time in trapping and target shooting. He spent two weeks doing dental work at Fort Sidney and started practice in Cheyenne in November, 1874, remaining there until the following year. In 1878 he began his career as exhibition marksman.

Another star of the first Wild West was Captain Adam H. Bogardus, billed — surprisingly, considering his long rivalry with the quarrelsome Carver — as the "Champion Pigeon Shot of America." Bogardus has a unique claim to distinction — he eliminated the original "stool pigeon." "Pigeon shot" described a marksman who shot live pigeons, usually passenger pigeons, lured to the target trap by a captive bird tied to a stool — the origin of the term "stool pigeon." Bogardus deplored the slaughter and began to use spring traps, triggered to throw out glass balls, in his matches. In the Wild West he used the Ligowsky clay pigeon. His methods standardized trap shooting, but came too late to save the passenger pigeon from extinction.

Bogardus was born in Albany County, New York, September 17, 1833. He came to Illinois in 1856 and became a market shooter at Elkhart, Logan County. He is still remembered in Elkhart: Bogardus Day featured the Illinois Sesquicentennial observance there in 1968. Bogardus won the Illinois championship from Abe Kleinman; Ira Paine, champion wingshot, conceded the national title to Bogardus in 1871; in 1878 Bogardus defeated Aubrey Coventry, England's champion, at Brighton. Four sons of Bogardus (Eugene, Peter, Edward, and Adam, Jr.), all expert shots, appeared with·him in the Wild West and in other exhibitions. Adam Bogardus was a partner in the second season of Buffalo Bill's Wild West, but withdrew in 1885.[12]

The first rehearsal of the show was at Colville (later Columbus), Nebraska, where Cody's insistence on authenticity in every detail nearly caused disaster. The Deadwood stagecoach he had obtained from Luke Voorhees, manager of the Cheyenne and Black Hills Stage Line, was drawn by a team of almost unbroken mules with a veteran driver, Fred Mathews, at the reins. When Major Frank North's Pawnees charged with a war whoop and shooting of blank cartridges, the mules bolted. The runaway continued around the hippodrome track, to the great distress of the mayor and councilmen, who were first among many distinguished guests to ride the Deadwood stage-coach in the show.

Major Frank North suggested that what was needed was more illusion and less realism — some worn-out hack horses and old Indians with less ambition. Major North himself was one element of the realism. He had commanded expeditions of Pawnee Scouts since 1864, notably in 1869 with the Fifth U. S. Cavalry, of which Cody was chief of scouts. The exploits of Major North and his Pawnee Scouts had become legendary by 1883.

There were others in that first company destined for future billing. North brought along as interpreter Gordon William Lillie, a teacher in the industrial school of the Pawnee agency, later to be known variously as Major Lillie, Pawnee Bill, and "the White Chief of the Pawnees."

A North Platte boy who had been a hero-worshiper of Cody begged to go along. Johnny Baker later became an expert marks-man, billed as the Cowboy Kid. Also from the North Platte area was Buck Taylor, soon listed as "King of the Cowboys" and subject of several of Colonel Prentiss Ingraham's dime novels. Others were Jim Bullock, steer rider; Jim Lawson, roper; Colonel Tom Wilson, and George Clother.

From his Theatrical Combination Cody recruited John M. Burke as general manager and Jule Keene as treasurer. Burke called himself Arizona John and "Major," neither for any ascertainable reason, and gained reputation as one of the world's great press agents. His writing featured sentences so overloaded with polysyllabic adjectives that they never arrived anywhere.

Thus Cody had a staff experienced in show business, if not in the new-type venture. In that period traveling companies and resident companies playing drama (they never admitted it was melodrama) were organized either as stock companies or as combinations. A stock company offered a repertory of plays — if billed for a week in a one-night-stand size town it might offer a different play each night. Thus a stock company was made up of actors capable of playing the "stock" roles in many plays — leading man, leading lady, character man, comedian, "heavy," or villain, soubrette, ingenue, and a few more who might play bit parts, and also take tickets, or act as treasurer, press agent, or advance man.

A combination was a company put together for a particular play, often built around a star as was the Buffalo Bill Combination. Booking agents were unknown, and the advance man seldom got far ahead if he had to come back to play bit parts or take tickets, so the combination often had a second play in reserve in case he came up with two or more days in a one-night-stand town. Both kinds of companies sought actors with specialties for between-the-acts use, and the Buffalo Bill Combination had shooting and roping exhibitions and other entertainment that carried over into the Wild West show. Usually an entire season was devoted to one play, such as *The Scouts of the Prairie, The Scouts of the Plains, The Red Right Hand, Life on the Border, The Prairie Waif,* and more of the kind, with occasional use of last year's play, or other earlier play, as an alternate.

The Wild West, Hon. W. F. Cody and Dr. W. F. Carver's Rocky Mountain and Prairie Exhibition opened at the Omaha Fair Grounds May 19, 1883.[13] Besides the attack on the Deadwood stagecoach, the show included many acts that were to become standard: the Pony Express, bucking broncos in "Cow-Boys' Fun," roping and riding wild Texas steers, much shooting, and many races. The closing spectacle was "A Grand Hunt on the Plains," with buffalo, elk, deer, mountain sheep, wild horses, and longhorns.

Carver had an off day in his shooting, perhaps because of too much celebrating prior to the opening, so Cody tried his hand at the glass

[13]William E. Deahl, Jr., "Nebraska's Unique Contribution to the Entertainment World," *Nebraska History,* XLIX (Autumn, 1968), 283-297. Deahl notes that the opening advertised for May 17 was postponed to May 19 because of rain.

balls. His performance was so successful that his act became a regular part of the show. The show had no tentage and no lighting. An attempt at a night show with bonfires, flares, and rockets flopped, so the show settled for afternoon engagements at fairgrounds and similar arenas during its first season's tour. It played Springfield, Illinois, and Chicago, then went to Boston, Newport, and Coney Island. Nate Salsbury saw the show there and found that "they had not developed my ideas in putting it together at all" and termed it "a ghastly failure."

That was exaggeration. One indication of its success is that it soon spewed a host of imitators. The *Hartford Courant* declared it "the best open-air show ever seen. . . . The real sight of the whole thing is, after all, Buffalo Bill. . . . Cody was an extraordinary figure and sits on a horse as if he were born to the saddle. His feats of shooting are perfectly wonderful. . . . He has, in this exhibition, out-Barnumed Barnum."

Of course Cody did not have a better show than Barnum, and he could not shoot as well as Carver, but he was a showman, one of America's greatest. That was recognized by almost everyone except those closest to him — his successive partners. Carver never saw it; they soon parted, and Carver spent the rest of his life hating Buffalo Bill. Salsbury looked upon Cody as a figurehead and himself as running the show, although happily Salsbury was content to stay out of the limelight and let Bill be the star. Pawnee Bill Lillie in later years also disparaged Cody's showmanship.

No one of the three, Doc, Nate, or Pawnee Bill, ever got it into his head that Buffalo Bill was all that press-agentry made him out to be, and perhaps a little more. This is another curious instance of Cody's modesty and reticence in discussing his exploits, traits of character noted by army officers under whom he had served. As scout for the Indian-fighting army, he won praise in their official reports. Even today Buffalo Bill typifies the Wild West to more people in more parts of the world than any other individual.

William Frederick Cody was born February 26, 1846, at LeClaire, Scott County, Iowa, the son of Isaac Cody and Mary Ann (Laycock) Cody. Will attended short sessions of several schools, most of them organized by his father, who dabbled in politics. The family moved to Kansas in 1854 and as soon as that territory was opened to settlement, Isaac Cody filed a claim in Salt Creek Valley near Fort Leavenworth. He was stabbed while speaking for the Free State cause, but recovered and was a member of the unrecognized Topeka Legislature and one of the founders of Grasshopper Falls (now Valley Falls). His death in 1857, three years later, was attributed by his family to the stabbing.

After his father's death young Will went to work as mounted messenger for the freighting firm of Majors & Russell (later Russell, Majors & Waddell), at first between Leavenworth and Fort Leavenworth, afterward on wagon-train trips across the Plains. He was a messenger for the army supply train in charge of Lewis Simpson when Lot Smith's party burned it during the "Mormon War." Cody rode Pony Express for Russell, Majors & Waddell and is credited with the third longest emergency ride of that short-lived venture while on the division headed by the notorious Joseph A. Slade.

In the early Civil War years Cody joined the Red-legged Scouts and other irregular militia commands, one of which he admits was a "jay-hawking enterprise," meaning a band of horse thieves. When he became eighteen years of age in 1864, he enlisted as a private in the veteran Seventh Kansas Volunteer Cavalry, serving in campaigns against Confederate generals Bedford Forrest and Sterling Price.

While stationed in St. Louis, Cody met Louisa Frederici and they were married in 1866. He tried hotel-keeping in his old Salt Creek Valley neighborhood with little success, then went West, worked irregularly as scout and guide, tried to found a town called Rome, and worked on railroad building. During 1867-1868 he contracted to supply buffalo meat for construction workers on the Union Pacific, Eastern Division (soon renamed Kansas Pacific) and it was then that he became known as Buffalo Bill.

In carrying dispatches over a long route through hostile Indian country, he came to the attention of Lieutenant General Philip H. Sheridan who employed Cody as chief of scouts for the 5th U. S. Cavalry. His continuous employment as scout for more than four years was exceptional, since scouts usually were hired for a specific expedition. Cody took part in sixteen Indian fights, including the defeat of the Cheyennes at Summit Springs under Brevet Major General Eugene A. Carr. General Carr praised Cody for his "extraordinarily good services as trailer and fighter" and noted that his markmanship was "very conspicuous." In asking an increase in pay for Cody from the War Department, Carr said, "I hope to retain him

Skeptics, even including his sometime partners, gave Colonel Cody little credit
for his handling business details of show business, but here is photographic
evidence that he took part in route planning as he is caught at work
with a Baltimore & Ohio Rail Railroad time-table in hand.
Courtesy of the Buffalo Bill Memorial Museum, Lookout Mountain, Colorado.

as long as I am engaged in this duty."

Shortly after Summit Springs, Cody was accompanied on an expedition by Edward Zane Carroll Judson, who used the pen-name Ned Buntline as a prolific writer of dime novels. In 1869 Ned Buntline made Buffalo Bill the hero of a sensational story that was later dramatized. General Sheridan specified Cody as guide for hunting parties of notables, including the Earl of Dunraven, a group of newspapermen, and the Grand Duke Alexis of Russia in a widely publicized hunt in 1872. Buntline sought to capitalize on the fame of his hero and persuaded Cody to appear with him on the melodrama stage in Chicago. The venture proved successful, but Cody broke with Buntline after the first year and continued with Texas Jack (John B. Omohundro) and his old friend Wild Bill (James B. Hickok). (Ned Buntline's part in the Buffalo Bill legend has been greatly exaggerated; he wrote only four original Buffalo Bill dime novels and was never publicity agent or ghost writer for Cody.)

Buffalo Bill appeared on the melodrama stage eleven seasons before he launched his Wild West on the Omaha Fair Grounds, May 19, 1883. There is some evidence that his offering during this early period was sometimes called a "Wild West show." In his first, and most authentic autobiography, published in 1879, Cody wrote, "I purpose to go next season on a theatrical tour [of England,] having been urged to do so by my many friends abroad." But in any event, the experience he had led directly to the full, outdoor exhibitions, which have made his name synonymous with Wild West shows.

During his years in the theater Cody spent many of his summers guiding hunting parties, and two of them as army scout. In 1876 he was back with the Fifth Cavalry and at Hat Creek killed Yellow Hand (more accurately Hay-o-wei, or Yellow Hair), the much-publicized "first scalp for Custer." The facts of this encounter are authenticated by official reports and eye-witness accounts, but Cody's almost immediate exploitation of it provoked questioning. Obviously J. V. Arlington's melodrama *The Red Right Hand; or, Buffalo Bill's First Scalp for Custer*, which Cody played with his fellow scout Captain Jack Crawford during the season of 1876-1877, was not strictly accurate historically. Cody himself said of it that it was "a five-act play without head or tail, and it made no difference at which act we commenced the performance."

This informal type of theatrical entertainment could have led easily to the outdoor show; there were horses on stage, a trained donkey is mentioned, shooting acts by Cody and other marksmen, fireworks, and, sometimes, genuine Indians. The plays were close to the dime novels, popular in the period, in titles as well as content. The first was *Scouts of the Prairie* by Ned Buntline, who probably based it on his most recent dime novel. It was succeeded by *Scouts of the Plains* by Fred G. Maeder, who had also dramatized Ned Buntline's first Buffalo Bill story. This lasted the scouts until 1876, with the aid of an anonymous alternate play called *Life on the Border.*

Buffalo Bill produced another timely play in 1877. Major Andrew S. Burt's *May Cody; or, Lost and Won* dealing with the Mormon War was presented soon after John D. Lee had been put to death for his part in the Mountain Meadows massacre. Colonel Prentiss Ingraham, who compiled more wordage in Buffalo Bill dime novels than any other writer, contributed the next two plays, *The Knights of the Plains; or Buffalo Bill's Best Trail,* and *Buffalo Bill at Bay; or, The Pearl of the Prairies.* One of the most popular of Buffalo Bill melodramas was *The Prairie Waif,* by John A. Stevens. Others, authorship not traced, were *Vera Vance; or, Saved from the Sioux, From Noose to Neck,* and *Twenty Days; or Buffalo Bill's Pledge.*

The transition from such spectacles as these to an outdoor exhibition was not revolutionary. Cody reversed it two years after starting the Wild West by returning to the stage with Buck Taylor, his arena star, in a revival of *The Prairie Waif* for the season of 1885-1886. In 1892 Carver organized a company that put on an outdoor Wild West in afternoons and a stage melodrama *The Scout* at night.

Just how successful Cody and Carver were during the first season of the Wild West is unclear. Cody wrote his sister, Julia, that he had not made much money but that he had spent freely for advertising and facilities for the following season. Salsbury said Cody told him in Chicago in October that he would not go through another season with Carver. The break came when Carver proposed a winter tour. Cody refused, and the partners divided their assets when the show closed at Omaha. The parting was apparently amicable, but their "era of good feelings" did not last long.

Carver recruited as partner Captain Jack Crawford (John Wallace Crawford), the Poet Scout, and showed Nashville, Atlanta, Charleston, Montgomery, Mobile, New Orleans and other Southern cities. Crawford, a Civil War veteran, was a scout in 1876 and his captaincy derived from a militia company of Black Hills Rangers. Captain Jack remained on the stage with Cody until they quarreled, after which Crawford was quite as vituperative as Carver in discussing the erstwhile partner; however, Captain Jack did not eliminate verses highly laudatory of Buffalo Bill from successive printings of his book *The Poet Scout.*[14] The Carver and Crawford Wild West was still on the road May 3, 1885, when it was billed in St. Louis, but the advertisement is signed J. J. McCafferty, proprietor and manager, raising the question as to how much financial interest either had in the show.[15]

John Peter Altgeld, later a famed liberal governor of Illinois, drew up the contract under which Cody, Salsbury, and Bogardus carried on the show to be known as Buffalo Bill's Wild West — America's National Entertainment. Salsbury, born February 28, 1846, was just two days younger than Cody. Salsbury ran away from home at fifteen to join the Union Army in the Civil War. He was captured and imprisoned in Andersonville, started the study of law after the war, but was detoured to the stage by way of amateur theatricals. After an apprenticeship in stock companies, he organized his own company, "The Troubadours," with which he toured for twelve years, including a trip to Australia. He stayed with this troupe during the season of 1884 to keep the pot boiling for the Wild West.

However, he visited the lot in the spring, finding Cody "surrounded by a lot of harpies called old timers who were getting as drunk as he at his expense." He left a letter for Cody to read when he sobered up. There is persistent legendry that Nate limited Bill to one, or ten, or twelve drinks a day, which Bill took in the largest available glassware. The fact is that Cody promised, "This drinking surely ends today and your pard will be himself, and on deck all the time." The evidence indicates that Cody hewed to the line and that he never missed a performance because of being drunk — nor did he hesitate to notify Nate that "when the show is laid up for winter I am going to get on a drunk that is a drunk."

[14]Captain Jack Crawford [John Wallace Crawford], *The Poet Scout* (San Francisco: H. Keller & Company, 1879), and *The Poet Scout* (New York: Funk and Wagnall's, 1886), have entirely different introductions, each of which contains autobiographical matter, but nothing relating to his outdoor show experience.

[15]Thorp reproduces this ad in "Doc Carver vs. Buffalo Bill," p. 33, but misdates it as 1884 in his biography in which there are only two passing references to the "McCafferty brothers" as partners "staying always in the background." See Thorp, *Spirit Gun*, pp. 15, 160. Thorp had exclusive access to the Carver papers, but in many cases erred in the use of them, making it difficult to estimate the importance of the Carver shows.

The 1884 season opened with an all-star cast of Western notables, headed by Major Frank North, who was now Cody's ranching partner. Advertised as guest star was Captain David L. Payne, the Oklahoma Boomer, who probably made few if any appearances, for he was busy most of the summer trying to force the opening of Oklahoma to settlement. He died that fall. *Buck Taylor, King of the Cowboys,* a dime novel by Prentiss Ingraham, is called the first publication with a cowboy hero. William Levi Taylor, known as Buck, was long a star in Buffalo Bill's Wild West. Another was Con Groner, "the Cow-Boy Sheriff of the Platte." One of his claims to fame was that of having rounded up Doc Middleton's gang of outlaws. At a later date Doc Middleton also appeared in the Wild West.

Another occasional guest star was Dr. Frank Powell, called White Beaver, onetime army surgeon, onetime partner of Buffalo Bill in a patent medicine business, dime novel hero, exhibition marksman, and occasionally a practicing physician. There were others. John Y. Nelson, scout, guide, and interpreter, with his Sioux wife and five children in Indian costume, dominated many a group picture of Wild West personnel. Johnny Baker, "the Cowboy Kid," who had been with the show from the beginning, and would stay to the end, was moving along toward stardom as marksman.

In Chicago one audience was counted at 41,448 — tremendous for those days. In New York the riding acts and roping were praised. Bad luck came at Hartford when Frank North was thrown and trampled by a horse. He died of his injuries the following spring, March 14, 1885. The show was not doing too well, and the partners decided to play the World's Industrial and Cotton Exposition in New Orleans through the winter. A steamboat was engaged to take the show there, playing stops along the way from Cincinnati. At Rodney Landing, Mississippi, there was a collision with another river boat and Cody wired Salsbury, "Outfit at bottom of river, what do you advise." Salsbury, ready to go on stage with his Troubadours at Denver, hesitated only while the orchestra repeated an overture before replying, "Go to New Orleans, reorganize, and open on your date." Cody salvaged the Deadwood coach, band wagon, and horses, and rounded up buffalo, elk, wagons, and equipment within eight days, to open on time.

He deserved better than the forty-four consecutive days of rain that plagued the show. One day only nine tickets were sold, but Cody

Group of Buffalo Bill's Wild West cowboys, Paris, France, 1905. Left to right,
first row: Johnnie Franz; Billie Burns; Joe Esquivel, chief of cowboys; Col. Cody;
Antonio (Tony) Esquivel, champion vaquero; Fred Burns;
Ed Phillips; William McCloud; second row; That Sowder; Tom Webb;
Ed Dollard; Vill Merrill; Robert Mason; Billie Craver; Burt Schenck;
Andrew Bellknap; third row; Silas Compton, called Si or Cy; Clarency Baker;
Thomas J. Isbell; Harry Brannan. Sowder was national champion bronc rider,
Cheyenne, 1900, and also in Denver, 1901 and 1902, and joined the show
in 1903. Craver rode Steamboat at Cheyenne Frontier Days, 1904, and joined the
show next year. Compton was arena director in London in 1892 and chief of cowboys,
1910. Isbell, a veteran of Roosevelt's Rough Riders (Troop L, 1st U. S.
Volunteer Cavalry), was wounded in the fight at Las Guasimas, Cuba,
June 25, 1898, and joined the show in 1899. William McCloud may be the
"Tex" McCloud billed as the champion roper of Idaho in the Jess Willard-Buffalo Bill
show of 1917. Brannan was champion bronco buster, Cheyenne, 1904.
Photograph by James E. Hunt, Nottingham; Reproduced in Paris program, 1905.
Courtesy of the State Historical Society of Colorado.

said, "If nine people came out in all this rain to see us, we'll show," and they did. In all this gloom there was one bit of good luck, not at all recognized at the time. Sells Brothers Circus was also showing in New Orleans, and some of its performers visited the Wild West lot. Among them were Mr. and Mrs. Frank Butler. Mrs. Butler was known professionally as Annie Oakley.

Annie Oakley was the greatest personality developed by the Wild West shows. Even yet her name rings loud and clear in American folklore with only slight aid from comic books, television exposure, and the Rodgers and Hammerstein *Annie Get Your Gun*, with songs by Irving Berlin. She was born August 13, 1860, fifth child of Jacob and Susan Moses. She was christened Phoebe Ann, but the Ann became Annie. Later she altered her last name to Mozee. At six her father died; at eight she shot a squirrel through the head with the aid of a porch railing as rest for a long rifle; at fifteen she was supplying game to a hotel in Cincinnati. When Frank Butler came along in an exhibition shooting act, issuing the usual challenge to local experts, the hotelkeeper bet on Annie, and Annie won. Frank and Annie were married a year later, June 22, 1876, and took the road, playing stock companies and variety. It was at this time that Annie picked the stage name Oakley out of thin air. When they visited Buffalo Bill's Wild West they liked what they saw and applied for a job.[16]

Cody and Salsbury were doubtful. They were short of funds and long on shooting acts, even though Bogardus had pulled out. Butler proposed to put their act on trial. They joined at Louisville early in 1885. She put on her act and was hired in fifteen minutes.

She claimed no championships, and her record book shows that she was beaten occasionally, but no one ever excelled her in showmanship. Dexter Fellows, veteran press agent, explained:

> She was a consummate actress, with a personality that made itself felt as soon as she entered the arena. . . . Her entrance was always a very pretty one. She never walked. She tripped in, bowing, waving, and wafting kisses. Her first few shots brought forth a few screams of fright from the women, but they were soon lost in round after round of applause. It was she who set the audience at ease and prepared for the continuous crack of firearms which followed.[17]

[16]Courtney Ryley Cooper, *Annie Oakley, Woman at Arms* (New York: Duffield and Company, 1927); Annie Fern Swartwout, *Missie* (Blanchester, Ohio: Brown Publishing Company, 1947); Walter Havighurst, *Annie Oakley of the Wild West* (New York: Macmillan Company, 1954).
[17]Dexter W. Fellows and Andrew A. Freeman, *This Way to the Big Show* (New York: Halcyon House, 1936), p. 73.

Her customary spot was No. 2 on the program, just after the grand entry. She probably was not photogenic, as her pictures vary from plain to pretty, but in the arena she was "America's sweetheart."

No more prim a little lady ever traveled the show circuits. She spent most of her spare time at embroidery, at which she was almost as expert as with a rifle. Some consider her to have been a tightwad. She drank no liquor but occasionally took a glass of beer — when someone else was buying. One of her rifle scores (Tiffin, Ohio, 1884) was 943 out of 1,000 glass balls, which is 94.3 per cent. A shotgun score (Cincinnati, 1885) was 4,772 out of 5,000 in nine hours, figuring 95.4 per cent. She frequently used cards thrown into the air as targets. One such card that she used was about five by two inches with a picture of Annie at one end and a heart-shaped target at the other. Such targets were thrown into the audience as souvenirs. "Annie Oakley" became show slang for a pass or complimentary ticket because such tickets were punched full of holes for identification when the receipts were counted.

Annie Oakley was billed, with surprising restraint, as the "Celebrated Shot, who will illustrate her dexterity in the use of Fire-arms," and as "The Peerless Wing and Rifle Shot." A more lasting designation, "Little Sure Shot," was conferred on her by Sitting Bull.

Sitting Bull made a tour in 1884 and it was probably in a St. Paul theatre that he saw Annie Oakley. They met after the show and exchanged pictures. The photograph of Annie saved the day when John M. Burke was trying to sign up Sitting Bull for appearance in Buffalo Bill's Wild West. Sitting Bull's previous tour had been an unhappy one, and he was reluctant to try another, but when Burke spotted the photograph and told him "Little Sure Shot" was with the show, Sitting Bull signed a contract June 6, 1885, agreeing to appear for four months at $50 a week and a bonus of $125. He got a chance to tell his troubles to the President in Washington, and was lionized in Canada. The often-reproduced photographs of Buffalo Bill and Sitting Bull were taken by William Notman in Montreal. Sitting Bull sold photographs and autographs and was generous in giving his money to newsboys, bootblacks, and other urchins who hung about the showgrounds. He could not understand such poverty in the midst of the white man's wealth. It was his only season in show business, but there is no indication that he did not enjoy it. When he left, Cody gave him a trick horse to which he had become attached and a white

Annie Oakley, dubbed "Little Sure Shot" by Sitting Bull, was star performer in Buffalo Bill's Wild West from the time she joined the show in 1885. This rare and phony publicity photograph, showing the Darke County, Ohio, country girl shooting rabbits, was probably sold on the show during the 1887 London engagement.
Amon Carter Museum Collection.

sombrero, size eight. When one of his relatives put it on, Sitting Bull rebuked him, saying, "My friend Long Hair gave me this hat. I value it very highly, for the hand that placed it upon my head had a friendly feeling for me."[18]

Cody, while stuck in the mud at New Orleans, could hardly have guessed that within a few months he would be making a triumphal tour of Canada with Sitting Bull and Annie Oakley as his stars. Johnny Baker was first advertised that year as the "Cow-boy Kid." Antonio Esquivel was featured as outstanding horseman. Buck Taylor and Con Groner still had top billing.

At midsummer the triumph still seemed far away. In New England the Buffalo Bill show tangled with Carver's Wild West. Each sued the other for libel; there were attachments and court hearings. What it was all about is unclear and perhaps not worth untangling, but Salsbury eventually effected a settlement out of court. Carver claimed he had won his case but lost his show. Apparently Carver was abandoned at this time by both J. J. McCafferty, advertised as proprietor and manager of his show, and Captain Jack Crawford.

There was other competition. Carver's advertising for New Haven in July, 1885, used only his own name and denounced imitators of his "original" Wild West, naming six in a "list of failures." Heading the list of course was Buffalo Bill, who was not failing as fast as Carver hoped. Another was W. C. Coup, a great name in the outdoor show world. William Cameron Coup (1837-1895) reputedly persuaded P. T. Barnum to go into the circus business in 1870 and to make it a railroad show. Their partnership ended in 1875, and a circus historian lists thereafter Coup's Equescurriculum, and for 1884, Coup and Carver's Wild West. This would seem to suggest another Carver partnership squabble. Coup never again had quite the success he had had with Barnum, but his name was usually on some kind of show until his death.

The same historian names "J. R. Cortine's, W. Hennessy, Prop." as an 1885 show, but is of no help in identifying Skakel & Martin or Fargo & Company of Carver's list. Quite possibly all three were the failures Carver called them. Last on Carver's blacklist is Captain E. E. Stubbs, who as "champion wing-shot of the West" challenged

---

[18]Stanley Vestal [Walter S. Campbell], *Sitting Bull, Champion of the Sioux* (Boston: Houghton Mifflin, 1932), p. 256. The contract for Sitting Bull's appearance in Buffalo Bill's Wild West is printed in *Middle Border Bulletin*, III (Autumn, 1943), 1-2.

Carver to matches in 1878 and 1885, the second of which challenges resulted in a brawl. Stubbs is not identified as having tried a Wild West show. Carver missed naming the Hart & Schofield Indian Show, which is said to have been on the road about 1885. With the record number of fifty outdoor shows reported for 1885, there may have been other Wild West shows; however, neither Cody nor Carver had experienced enough success thus far to stimulate imitation.[19]

But Cody was coming up fast. From the start Buffalo Bill's Wild West had sought long engagements in large cities, not having railroad equipment at this time to make a series of one-day stands possible. During 1886 the show stayed six months at Erastina, a summer resort operated by Erastus Wiman on Staten Island. The show was still long on shooting acts. Lillian Smith, fifteen-year-old rifle shot from Coleville, California, could break 495 out of 500 glass balls. Seth Clover used marbles as targets. The rivalry of Annie Oakley and Johnny Baker was becoming an asset. Many spectators supposed it was set up for Annie to win, but Johnny admitted that he never was able to beat her. Buffalo Bill himself was headlined as "a practical all-around shot." As for his scores, he wrote his sister during the first year of the show, "I broke 87 glass balls out of one hundred thrown from a trap 21 yards rise with a shotgun riding a horse at full speed. I have broken 76 out of a hundred with a rifle running full speed."

Doc Middleton, the Nebraska bandit, and his nemesis Sheriff Con Groner are both said to have been in the show this year. Jim Mitchell fought the famous bucking black mare Dynamite. James Willoughby, known as Jim Kid, rode the bucker White Emigrant on which he had won the Montana championship in 1884.

These notables were viewed by other notables from the stands — General Sherman, Mark Twain, P. T. Barnum, Thomas A. Edison, and Mrs. Custer, widow of the General slain at the Little Big Horn. All had words of praise for the show, and they were not alone. In one July week the attendance totaled 193,960.

Cody and Salsbury decided to try for the big time and made a deal with Adam Forepaugh for a winter exhibition in Madison Square Garden. Steele Mackaye, a notable name in theatre, wrote a scenario,

---

[19]Chindahl, *History of the Circus*, has an appendix, "A Partial List of American Circuses and Menageries," including some Wild West shows; other details from May, *From Rome to Ringling*, passim; and Thorp, *Spirit Gun*, passim. A survey in the *Wall Street Journal*, June 6, 1953, says the "high mark in number of circuses was set in 1885 when the country had more than 50."

or "drama without words," for a pageant-like production called *The Drama of Civilization*, with scenic effects by Matt Morgan, and mechanical effects by Nelse Waldron, inventor of a double stage, or revolving stage, used in Mackaye's Madison Square Theatre. Lew Parker, stage manager, devised a cyclone to blow down Deadwood City of the Black Hills. He had discovered a ventilator and ordered three enlarged copies of the fan, five feet in diameter. The electric fan was as yet unknown; the ventilators were driven by steam power, piped from across the street. Dried leaves dropped in front of the fan effected a quite realistic cyclone. Louis E. Cooke, Forepaugh's polysyllabic press agent, hailed "a gigantic new era and departure in colossically realistic scenic production."[20]

Both Cody and Salsbury had long been ambitious to show the Wild West in Europe. The opportunity came with an offer to take part in the American Exhibition planned for Queen Victoria's Golden Jubilee in 1887 in London. The State Line steamship *State of Nebraska* was engaged, and the on-board count of the "company of more than two hundred" totaled eighty-three saloon passengers, thirty-eight steerage passengers, and ninety-seven Indians. Livestock included 180 horses, eighteen buffalo, ten elk, ten mules, five Texas steers, four donkeys, and two deer. After unloading at Gravesend, three trains took the show to Earl's Court, London, where camp was set up. Notables of stage and politics, Henry Irving, Ellen Terry, Mary Anderson, Justin McCarthy, and William E. Gladstone visited the camp, and on May 5, four days before the opening, a special performance was given for Albert Edward, Prince of Wales — who became King Edward VII — and his royal party. This resulted in a command performance for Queen Victoria, her first appearance at a public entertainment since the death of her consort, Prince Albert.

Another command performance was given June 20 for the Jubilee guests, and it was on this occasion that the Deadwood coach carried four kings in addition to the Prince of Wales, with Buffalo Bill as driver. The kings were Leopold II of Belgium, Christian IX of Denmark, George I of Greece, and Albert of Saxony. Said the Prince of Wales, an experienced poker player:

"Colonel, you never held four kings like these before."

[20]Lew Parker, *Odd People I Have Met* (privately printed, n. d.), pp. 37-39.

"I've held four kings," said Cody, "but four kings and the Prince of Wales makes a royal flush, such as no man ever held before."[21]

The interest of royalty in the Wild West was only exceeded by that of the common people. Lew Parker records that on Easter Monday 83,000 passed the turnstiles of the Exhibition Grounds. The crush of people threatened to collapse a viaduct until quick-thinking showmen sent a band to draw them off. Despite the attraction of a Cyclorama of New York Harbor contributed by Frédéric Auguste Bartholdi, sculptor of the Statue of Liberty, the American Exhibition was dominated by Buffalo Bill's Wild West. *The Times* recorded that Cody "found himself the hero of the London season," and Marshall P. Wilder, American dwarf comedian and writer, declared that

> the greatest, most unapproachable, thoroughly howling success that America ever sent to London was Buffalo Bill. I must express my pride and delight, as an American, at the figure Bill cut in society. . . . Bill always knew exactly what to do and say . . . always kept his heart and manners in good working order.[22]

The show itself was greatly enlarged. Steele Mackaye's scenic effects were applied to an arena enclosed by a track one-third mile in circumference. William Sweeney's Cowboy Band of thirty-six mounted musicians gave a half-hour concert of classical and popular music preceding the performance. The spectacles included "Custer's Last Fight", the attack on the settler's cabin, a buffalo hunt, and the run of the Deadwood stagecoach. The square dance on horseback featured Emma Lake, sometimes billed as Emma Lake Hickok, daughter of Agnes Lake, circus owner married to Wild Bill shortly before he was killed in Deadwood. Emma taught her horse to jump to music and to stand on his hind legs to bow. The all-star cast included Annie Oakley, Lillian Smith, and Johnny Baker in shooting acts; Buck Taylor, King of the Cowboys; Antonio Esquivel, top rider; Mustang Jack, Jim Kidd, recently married to Lillian Smith; Jim Mitchell; Mrs. Georgia Duffy, rough rider of Wyoming; the veteran Con Groner; and many more.

The show played London from May 9 to October 31. Annie Oakley, who had also been lionized in London, quit the show at this time to accept an invitation to Berlin from Crown Prince Wilhelm — the

[21]William Frederick Cody, *Story of the Wild West and Camp-Fire Chats* (Philadelphia: Historical Publishing Company, 1888), pp. 742-743, although I like the one in which Cody calls the prince the Royal Joker.
[22]Marshall P. Wilder, *The People I've Smiled With* (Akron: Werner Company, 1899), pp. 108-121.

The "Wild West" at the Great American Exhibition. *The London Illustrated News*,
June 18, 1887, pp. 682-683, insisted on calling the buffalo hunted by Buffalo Bill
in foreground "bison," but throws us off by identifying the elk, or wapiti,
being roped in background as "wapiti deer."
Amon Carter Museum Collection.

Buffalo Bill's Cowboy Band, William Sweeney, conductor, 1887-1913.
A London newspaper in 1887 commented that they "upset all one's previous
ideas about the correct costume of musicians, but they play with spirit."
They wore gray shirts, slouched hats, and mocassins, rode matched
horses on parade, and played a half-hour concert of classical music preceding the
performance. This photograph was taken during the third tour of England, about 1904.
Photograph by James E. Hunt, Nottingham; Courtesy of the
Buffalo Bill Memorial Museum, Lookout Mountain, Colorado.

Kaiser of World War I. Buffalo Bill's Wild West went on to Birmingham November 5. At Manchester in December a *Depiction of American Pioneer History* was modeled on the indoor show at Madison Square Garden the previous winter. An added scene was a prairie fire stampeding animals and imperiling an emigrant train, effected by burning a small amount of grass behind a steam curtain some distance in front of it. The Manchester engagement continued from December 17 to April 30, but slowing business persuaded Cody and Salsbury to return home. The final performance at Hull May 5 drew crowds on numerous excursion trains. The show sailed next day and on arrival at New York opened another engagement at Erastina.

SECOND EPISODE—
The Real Wild West: If Any Seek It, They Defraud

Such a degree of success deserved instant imitation, and got it from Adam Forepaugh (1831-1890), one of the great names in circus business. He had built a butcher business into livestock dealing, and a sale of horses involved him in a circus partnership. In 1865 he built a permanent circus building in Philadelphia, and after a successful winter, took his show on the road in the spring. He soon became a top competitor and his use of the punning "4-paw" aided his publicity, particularly among cartoonists. He outsmarted Barnum by leasing Madison Square Garden, but compromised and the two shows were combined for the New York run.

Captain Bogardus put on a Wild West for a week in the 1887 spring show and shortly Adam Forepaugh's New and Greatest All-feature Show added a spectacle of "Custer's Last Rally" to its "4-paw's Wild West" feature. In 1888 the show was termed the Forepaugh and Wild West Combination, and sometimes in reverse as the Combined Wild West and Forepaugh Exhibitions, while the Custer spectacle was billed as "The Progress of Civilization," apparently to suggest Mackaye's pageant for Buffalo Bill.

Doc Carver's part in all this is not entirely clear, although he was heavily featured in the 1888 program and in other advertising, and it was announced that he "appears at every exhibition of the Combined Wild West and Great Forepaugh Shows." The billing "Dr. Carver's Wild West" occurs only on a stock cut that may have been carried over from his previous show. The Wild West seems to be Forepaugh's, and not a merger with the former Carver show.

The only other top billing went to Adam Forepaugh, Jr., as "The Crown Prince of the Zoological World." He worked elephants and wild animals but gets a niche in circus history for his act in which he rode and drove thirty-nine horses. This was in 1890; in 1888 only thirty horses were advertised. He had also trained the Horse Blondin to walk a tight rope thirty feet from the ground. (The human Blondin was notable for crossing Niagara Falls on a tight rope.)

There was much in the Forepaugh Wild West that seems to imitate the Buffalo Bill show. "Carazo, the Female Crack Shot of the World" was a close approximation of Annie Oakley; there was a Cow-Boy Brass Band, and Round-Up Bob, champion trick rider and roper of Texas.

Doc Carver quit the show in the fall of 1888, but Forepaugh continued the Wild West combination through 1889, featuring the "Custer's Last Rally" spectacle. Adam Forepaugh, Sr., died January 22, 1890, and his show was bought by James A. Bailey and James E. Cooper. Bailey continued the name as a big show, with occasional breaks, and in 1896 formed the combination Forepaugh and Sells Brothers, a top ranked circus until 1911. The show's later reputation overshadowed Adam Forepaugh's contribution to the Wild West show, but his was the first big-time combination of circus and Wild West.

Another show destined for big time got its start in 1888 — the Pawnee Bill Historical Wild West Exhibition and Indian Encampment. Gordon W. Lillie (Pawnee Bill) had been an interpreter for the Pawnee Indians in the original Cody & Carver Wild West of 1883. Born in Bloomington, Illinois, February 14, 1860, Lillie received the equivalent of a high school education and was bookkeeper in his father's flour mill before the family moved to Wellington, Kansas. Striking out for himself at sixteen, he was trapper and cowboy before becoming secretary to the agent and teacher at the Pawnee Agency. His year with Buffalo Bill inspired his interest in show business, and in 1885 he took a troupe of Indians on tour with the Healy and Bigelow Medicine Show — medicine shows were big business in that period. Lillie was back with Buffalo Bill for the season of 1886.

Buffalo Bill's 1887 success had pointed up a bonanza for Wild West shows in Europe and Pawnee Bill was headed for an exposition sponsored by King Leopold II at Brussels, Belgium, when it was canceled by the death of Emperor Wilhelm I of Germany, March 9, 1888. Lillie had on his hands a company that included eighty-four Pawnee, Kaw, Wichita, Comanche, and Kiowa Indians; fifty cowboys and Mexican vaqueros, thirty trappers, hunters, and scouts; and 165 horses, mules, and buffalo. He quickly arranged a tour that included St. Joseph, Kansas City, Indianapolis, Columbus, and Philadelphia. The show got much favorable attention that was not reflected in the box office.

What happened next is confused by contradictory accounts. Annie Oakley and Frank Butler, returning from their European shooting tour, signed up with a Wild West show organized in Philadelphia. Too late they discovered that its cowboys had been recruited in Philadelphia and could not ride or perform. They discovered that Pawnee Bill had performers and no backers, so a merger was arranged. The Butlers did not name the original show they joined, but elsewhere it was stated that Charles M. Southwell of Philadelphia was partner or associate of Pawnee Bill at this time.

In five weeks at Gloucester Beach, New Jersey, 150,000 people saw the Pawnee Bill show, but a later tour of fairs in the South was unprofitable. A "billing war" with the Buffalo Bill show is said to have added to the disaster, but it seems unlikely it was decisive, as the Buffalo Bill show made only a very short tour after leaving Erastina. At Easton, Maryland, the Pawnee Bill show was attached by the sheriff.

Pawnee Bill, personally, was rescued by the Wichita Board of Trade, which employed him to head the Oklahoma Boomer movement as successor to David Payne. However, he was not called upon to lead any violent confrontation because there was hope of a legal settlement. Annie Oakley appeared in a variety act at Tony Pastor's Opera House in New York, and in a melodrama, *Deadwood Dick*.

The cowboy band in the Pawnee Bill show had been led by Buckskin Joe, who pulled out his bandsmen after they were not paid for two months. Buckskin Joe was Edward Jonathan Hoyt (1840-1918), who had been hunter, trapper, scout, Civil War soldier, and occasional showman. He organized Buckskin Joe's Realistic Wild West for one season (1892 or 1893) to play Boyden's Crescent Park in Providence, Rhode Island.[1]

Cody and Salsbury were ready for another invasion of Europe in 1889. This tour was to last four years. Again the *Persian Monarch* was engaged with landing at Le Havre and a long stand scheduled at the *Exposition Universale* in Paris. President Sadi-Carnot attended the opening, and while crowned heads were not as numerous as at Queen Victoria's Jubilee, the Shah of Persia, Nasr-ul-Deen attended, and Queen Isabella of Spain rode in the Deadwood coach.

The Paris program for *L'Ouest Sauvage de Buffalo Bill* followed the pattern that was becoming standardized — the Pony Express, the attack on the emigrant train, the Virginia quadrille on horseback,

---

[1]Glenn Shirley (ed.), *Buckskin Joe* (Lincoln: University of Nebraska Press, 1966), pp. 155-160, 166-168.

Johnny Baker, billed as "The Cow-boy Kid" and "The Celebrated Young
American Marksman," had become a feature attraction when
Buffalo Bill's Wild West first played Paris in 1889. "Petit Jean" repeated his
Paris triumph in 1905. Here he is shown giving an exhibition of his shooting skill
at Le Fusil de Chasse, the gun and hunting club of Paris.
Courtesy of the Buffalo Bill Memorial Museum, Lookout Mountain, Colorado.

Pawnee Bill's Wild West & Great Far East band and performers
posed in front of museum tents.
Courtesy of the Western History Collections, University of Oklahoma Library.

"l'amusement des cowboys," the attack on the Deadwood coach, Indian dances, the buffalo hunt, many races and many shooting acts. Annie Oakley was back in her usual spot early in the program, Johnny Baker and Buffalo Bill did their accustomed acts, while pistol shooting was demonstrated by M. C. L. Daly. Also featured were Buck Taylor, King of the Cowboys; Tony Esquivel, champion vaquero rider; Gabriel Dumont, exiled leader of Riel's Rebellion in Canada; John Y. Nelson and his Indian family; and there was a two-page tribute to "Vieux Charlie," the horse alleged to have carried Buffalo Bill 160 kilometres in nine hours, forty-five minutes. Old Charlie died on the way home from England in 1887 and was buried at sea.[2]

Rosa Bonheur, the most famous animal painter of her day — her "Horse Fair" has had a comeback in critical favor — spent much time on the show's back lot during its seven months run in Paris. Her painting of Buffalo Bill on horseback was used in books and show publicity, but she did at least seventeen others, mostly of buffalo and of mounted Indians.

After the Paris Exposition the Wild West toured southern France, including stops at Lyon and Marseille, then took ship for Barcelona. Buffalo Bill landed American Indians there 398 years after Columbus returned to Barcelona following his discovery of America, and Major John Burke played all the publicity angles. However, Barcelona was in partial quarantine for typhoid fever and influenza; Frank Richmond, the show's popular announcer, and four Indians died there; seven more ailing Indians were sent home, and Annie Oakley was seriously ill.

The tour of Spain was cut short, and the show moved on to Italy, opening in Naples January 26, 1890. In Rome a Wild West delegation was blessed by Pope Leo XIII. Buffalo Bill had to give up his ambition of playing the Colosseum, finding it too dilapidated, but a few weeks later used the Roman amphitheatre of Diocletian at Verona. The best break at Rome came when Don Onorto Herzog of Sermonetta, Prince of Teano, challenged the cowboys to ride his Cajetan stallions, which of course they did. After Florence, Bologna, and Milan, the Indians were photographed April 16 in Venice's gondolas.

---

[2] *L'Oueste Sauvage de Buffalo Bill* (Paris: Parrot et Cie., 1889).

Buffalo Bill Wild West Group aboard the S. S. *Princessen*, Bremen Line,
en route to Germany in 1891. Some of the members are:
(left to right) left front, seated, Fast Horse and Nellie, unidentified woman,
Mrs. Swan. Left, rear, nearest the ventilator; Sam Surrounded; to his right, David
Two Bull; and Wallace White Whirlwind (tentative).
Courtesy Fred B. Hackett, Chicago.

The 1890 tour continued to Innsbruck and the Tyrol to Munich, then to Vienna, Berlin, Dresden, Leipzig, Bonn, Coblentz, and Frankfurt, ending the season at Stuttgart.

Although Pawnee Bill had been balked in his plan for a show in Europe, others were trying it with varied success. When Black Elk missed the boat at the end of Buffalo Bill's first tour of England, he found temporary haven with Mexican Joe's Wild West in London — a show that left little other trace. Cody's old rival Doc Carver organized a Wild America show in partnership with Fred C. Whitney of Detroit, and landed it in Hamburg in June 1889. During the following two years Wild America showed in Berlin, Vienna, Budapest, Warsaw, Moscow, St. Petersburg, Helsingfors, and Stockholm. The Evil Spirit and Buffalo Bill crossed paths at Berlin in 1890, but both shows survived, and Carver took off for Australia after closing his season October 25.

Carver's principals included He Crow, Sioux chief, the scout Billy Garnett, Buckskin Frank McPartlin, and the Mexican roper, Indelicio Maldonado. At Melbourne Carver was persuaded to reorganize his troupe to give a melodrama, *The Scout*, in a theatre at night following an afternoon of Wild West in a stadium. Returning to the United States in 1892, he continued this program through 1893. Long after Carver's Wild West was forgotten, his diving horses were famous in the outdoor show world. For more than a quarter century after his death (August 31, 1927), the forty-foot high dive of horse and girl rider into a tank of water was an exhibition feature under direction of his daughter, Lorena Carver.[3]

Indians were popular in Europe, despite an occasional bad actor among them, and United States government policy generally favored this exposure to a wider view of the white man's world at a time when there was little other outside employment available to reservation Indians. Reformers, who believed Indians could be converted to white men's ways within a generation or two if native habits and customs were rigidly suppressed, took an opposing view. Buffalo Bill's Wild West came under fire during the 1890 tour when a defector, one White Horse, told a tale of cruelty and starvation to the *New York Herald*. Major Burke went into action at once, asking

[3]Thorp, *Spirit Gun*, pp. 177-218; for the diving horses see "Speaking of Pictures," *Life*, October 12, 1953, pp. 26-28; Peter M. Spackman, "Did You Ever See a Horse Fly?" *This Week*, January 10, 1959, pp. 1, 20-21; August 16, 1964, pp. 9, 11.

A novel scene at the Vatican. Buffalo Bill's Cowboy's and Red Men blessed by
Pope Leo XIII. From *Frank Leslie's Illustrated Newspaper*, April 12, 1890, p. 215.
Courtesy of the Library Company of Philadelphia.

the consul general, the secretary of legation at Berlin, and the consul at Hamburg to inspect the Indian camp. All three agreed that "they are certainly the best looking, and apparently the best fed Indians we have ever seen." The Paris edition of the *New York Herald* printed a handsome retraction, taking pride that their wide coverage made it possible that "stories wilder than the Wild West itself can be so promptly sat upon and refuted." This seemed conclusive, but Cody decided to clarify the matter with the Commissioner of Indian Affairs, so returned to America with the Indians, while the rest of the show wintered at Benfeld in Alsace-Lorraine.

When Cody landed in New York he was handed a telegram from Major General Nelson A. Miles, requesting him to come to Chicago. The Ghost Dance initiated by a Messiah known as Wovoka, or Jack Wilson, had excited the Indians of the Plains, and Miles feared an outbreak of Sioux. Cody agreed to attempt to "arrest" Sitting Bull, an idea that has been ridiculed by many commentators. But Cody knew Sitting Bull, had employed him in the show, and possibly could have persuaded the chief to come in and have a talk with Miles. Cody was unable to complete his mission, and Sitting Bull was killed when Indian police were sent to arrest him. The Wounded Knee fight followed, and Cody took the field as brigadier general of the Nebraska State Troops. Meanwhile Burke had taken the Wild West show Indians to Washington, cleared them with the Indian Bureau, and took them to Pine Ridge Agency, where they proved useful as peacemakers. Happily, the last of the Indian wars ended with little fighting.

So effective had been Cody's presentation of his case that he was permitted to enroll 100 Indians for his show in Europe. Among them were nineteen prisoners of war sent to Fort Sheridan, Illinois, including such leaders of the Ghost Dance movement as Kicking Bear, Short Bull, Lone Bull, Mash the Kettle, Scatter, and Revenge. Prominent among the peacemakers were Long Wolf, No Neck, Yankton Charlie, and Black Heart. The Indians left from Philadelphia on the Red Star steamship *Switzerland,* and landed at Antwerp, and joined the show at Strasbourg.[4]

Nate Salsbury had not been idle in the show's winter quarters. Faced with the possibility that the Indians might not return, he

[4]Cody's part in the Sioux War of 1890-1891 is told in more detail in Russell, *Lives and Legends of Buffalo Bill,* pp. 354-369.

put into effect his first idea of a show "that would embody the whole subject of horsemanship." From his headquarters in central Europe he recruited German and English soldiers, and a dozen Cossacks, who, added to United States soldiers, Argentine gauchos, Mexican vaqueros, cowboys and cowgirls — and, fortuitously, Indians — made a colorful and imposing Congress of Rough Riders of the World, a phrase that became firmly attached to the show's title from 1893 onward.[5] Quite probably it inspired Theodore Roosevelt's Rough Riders, the First United States Regiment of Volunteer Cavalry of the Spanish-American War.

The 1891 tour resumed the swing through Germany with stops at Karlsruhe, Mannheim, Mainz, Weisbaden, Cologne, Dortmund, Duisburg, Krefeld, Aachen, and Berlin. Kaiser Wilhelm II, whose interest in the American West had been sparked by his Potsdam schoolmate Poultney Bigelow, was a frequent visitor. German army officers studied the show's logistics — the continuous-procession unloading of flatcars, the rolling kitchens, the split-second campmaking methods developed by American outdoor shows to make possible their schedule of parade and two shows daily.

Queen Wilhelmina attended the performance in Holland after which the Wild West embarked at Antwerp to cross to England for a tour that included Liverpool, Manchester, Leeds, Sheffield, and Birmingham. A six-day stand at Cardiff, Wales, in September proved highly profitable. For the winter Steele Mackaye's indoor pageant was revived at Glasgow. Employment for this engagement of Sam Lockart's performing elephants and a group of Zulus brought to Europe by Henry M. Stanley presaged the Far East idea of a later period.

The 1892 season opened with a return to Earl's Court, London. Queen Victoria was eager to see the Cossacks, led by Prince Ivan Rostomov Macheradse, reputed descendant of Mazeppa, and a special showing was made up for Windsor Castle. The Cossacks proved far the most popular of the world rough riders with their colorful costumes and unorthodox feats of horsemanship, so much so that

---

[5] "Congress of Rough Riders of the World" probably was first used in programs and papers of 1893. A full-page ad in John Moses and Paul Selby, *The White City* (Chicago: Chicago World Book Company, 1893), p. 152, from internal evidence published before the Fair opened, features the show as "Congress of Nations — Hon. W. F. Cody." There are three variant printings of the 1893 program, all using the Rough Riders subtitle.

Plate II. Je Viens

The English version of this often-used poster, "I Am Coming,"
was produced as early as 1900. Frenchmen may have been promised "Je Viens" in
1889, and certainly were in 1905. Another version of this same poster is
"Here We Are," used in the United States.
Color lithograph. 28 x 40 inches.
Courtesy of the Buffalo Bill Historical Center, Cody, Wyoming.

they became a necessary feature of even the smallest of Wild West shows.

Cody landed in New York October 24, 1892, marking the end of his show's four-year tour of Europe. The following season was to be his biggest and best — some have said the most prosperous in outdoor show business — Buffalo Bill's Wild West and Congress of Rough Riders of the World at the World's Columbian Exposition in Chicago for 1893.

THIRD EPISODE—
Appearing Before the Crowned Heads of Europe

The World's Columbian Commission did not exactly invite Buffalo Bill to take part in the celebration of the 400th anniversary of the discovery of America, despite his subdued advertising emphasizing a Congress of Nations while spelling out Wild West in the smallest of type. In fact the Buffalo Bill show was not admitted to the exposition grounds. Fortunately, Nate Salsbury had the forethought to lease a lot near the main entrance between 62nd and 63rd streets. The World's Fair had a total gate of 27,539,041 and few of the visitors considered that they had seen the sights until they had also visited Buffalo Bill's Wild West. The show's profit was estimated at $700,000 to $1,000,000 for the season.

The only notable publicity stunt of the season was the Thousand-Mile Cowboy Race from Chadron, Nebraska, to the World's Fair. The idea of a race to test the endurance of the Western horse originated among Nebraska stockmen. Buffalo Bill got in on it by adding $500 to the purse on condition that the race finish in the Wild West arena. The run was made in thirteen days at an average of seventy-seven miles a day, and John Berry of Sturgis won. The ubiquitous ex-bandit, Doc Middleton, one of the entrants, failed to finish.

Major Burke is credited with being one of the greatest of publicity agents, but many fortuitous factors contributed to Wild West popularity in 1893. It was an heroic age. The United States, with a brief history to draw upon, had manufactured a democratic pantheon from such episodic figures as Paul Revere, Ethan Allen, Nathan Hale, Betsy Ross, and Molly Pitcher, whose reputations had been enhanced, and in a case or two created during recent Centennial observances. From Daniel Morgan and Daniel Boone, with a considerable boost from Fenimore Cooper's Leatherstocking, the frontier hero took over with such colorful protagonists as Davy Crockett and Kit Carson. It is perhaps no coincidence that the most dramatized minor incident in American history, Custer's Last Stand, took place in the Centennial Year of 1876. It was the subject for the spectacle in Buffalo Bill's Wild West in 1893.

The last of the Indian wars occurred in 1890-1891 — although no one yet knew it was the last — and Buffalo Bill had participated in it. At this same World's Fair, historian Frederick Jackson Turner noted that according to the 1890 census there was no longer a frontier and advanced his theory on "The Significance of the Frontier in American History." The Wild West had gone into history by 1893, with Buffalo Bill's Wild West left to commemorate it.

Buffalo Bill measured up to the ideal of the nineteenth century hero, and had the immense advantage that he looked the part. His record as army scout was actually better than his press agents made it out to be. They had not bothered to look it up. Why should they? The crowds that flocked to the Arena adjacent to the World's Fair came to see a dime-novel hero who was a living person and were worried not at all that the adventures described in the Buffalo Bill dime novels were entirely fictitious. We think of it as a simpler world than ours, but perhaps it was more complicated. There was then sharp division between the idealism and fantasy of the novel, and the play, and the "real world" that might be marked by monotony and boredom. That a William F. Cody could move freely back and forth between fact and fantasy could not be completely accepted — and so the nineteenth century hero was not taken altogether seriously. In fact there is a wealth of evidence that Cody did not take himself seriously.

There was one other reason for the popularity of the Wild West in Chicago in 1893 and that was its enthusiastic reception in Europe. There can be no doubt about the show's impact on Europe, or the continuing impression of the American West as a far-away land of romance and adventure. Probably no other show had been seen by as many of the crowned heads of Europe. Before World War I a wide-spread theory held that there was something called Western Civilization; that it had been developed in Europe; and Americans, despite much brash boasting of the merits of democracy, regarded culture as an import. They read the novels of Dickens, Thackeray, Scott, Dumas, and Hugo; they went to plays by Shakespeare, Sheridan, Tom Taylor, or Rostand; and if an American wrote either it was apt to come out *Ben-Hur, When Knighthood Was in Flower,* or *Francesca da Rimini.* High school students studied four years of

Plate III. Custer's Last Rally

was a spectacle in the "4-Paw's Wild West" section of Adam Forepaugh's
All Feature Show, 1887-1889. The show starred Dr. W. F. Carver the first two years,
and featured an elaborate pageant, "The Progress of Civilization."
Color lithograph. 26 x 39 inches.
Courtesy of the San Antonio Public Library, Hertzberg Circus Collection.

Latin, German, or possibly French; four years of English, which was mostly English literature; at least two years of science (Germany was considered tops in science and medicine); a year of ancient history, a year of medieval and modern history, a year of English history; and it often took an act of the legislature to add a year of American history and civics. Obviously the teachers had to take an annual Cook's tour of Europe to keep up with all this.

Buffalo Bill's Wild West had been the sensation of Europe for five of the last six years. Americans would accept that favorable verdict. So our simple, uncomplicated, nineteenth century hero, Buffalo Bill, became hero through forces that were neither simple nor uncomplicated.

What was the show that aroused all this enthusiasm? The program was very little different from that first revealed to the world in 1883, although the performance was much more expert and finished. The principal innovation was the Congress of Rough Riders of the World, introduced in an opening Grand Review featuring soldiers of America, England, France, Germany, and Russia. In a later number they performed military evolutions. In other events Syrian and Arabian horsemen, Cossacks, and Mexicans illustrated their styles of horsemanship. Just as circuses went in heavily for races on the hippodrome track, the Wild West interspersed three: one putting the Rough Riders in competition, one among Prairie, Spanish, and Indian girls, and a bareback race of Indian boys.

Annie Oakley had the number two spot, in accordance with the policy of getting women spectators used to shooting early in the show. Johnny Baker, "Celebrated Young American Marksman," was number eight, and Buffalo Bill's sharpshooting was number sixteen in an eighteen-event program. "Cowboy Fun," the predecessor of rodeo, was outlined as "picking objects from the ground, lassoing wild horses, riding the buckers." "Life customs of the Indians" was another feature.

The rest was Western pageant and spectacle. The Pony Express, a durable feature of the show, was demonstrated. The buffalo hunt billed "the last of the only known native herd." There was an attack on a "Prairie Emigrant Train Crossing the Plains" and capture of the Deadwood Mail Coach by the Indians, both of which were rescued by Buffalo Bill with his scouts and cowboys. At the beginning of the season the finale had been an attack on a settler's cabin, but a more climactic spectacle proved to be the "Battle of the Little Big Horn . . . showing with historical accuracy the scene of Custer's Last Charge."

The musical background for all these events came from the Cowboy Band led by William Sweeney, but there is no indication of an opening concert as later became the custom. "The Star-Spangled Banner" was listed as the overture even before it became the National Anthem, and its performance in open, outdoor entertainment was not yet customary. There is no indication of an aftershow, also called "concert" in outdoor show terminology.

No other names appeared on the program, unlike the later custom of listing everyone down to the last girl in the chorus line. Among those unmentioned were some top names of the Wild West. Vincenzo (sometimes Vincent) Orapeza was one of the top ropers of all time. He taught Will Rogers. Antonio Esquivel headed the vaqueros, and Jim Mitchell, the cowboys. John Y. Nelson was there with his Sioux family, and John Shangrau was in charge of the Indian "prisoners of war." Among the Indians were Kicking Bear, Short Bull, Plenty Horses, No Neck, Rocky Bear, Young-Man-Afraid-of-His-Horses, and Jack Red Cloud, son of the famous chief Red Cloud.

Its thrill cannot be recaptured in words. To many who saw it then, it was the top show of all time.

With all this success, almost unbroken for eight seasons, more imitators might be expected than show up in available records. Probably there were more, for shows came and went and changed their names in bewildering succession in the golden age of outdoor show business. Circus historians turn them up by chance in newspaper files, but no one can check all newspapers, and until *Billboard* began publication in 1896 there was no clearing house for show information. For example, Sutton's American Wild West and Roman Hippodrome played San Francisco April 19 to 29, 1890, possibly the first Wild West show on the Pacific coast, but that is about all we know about it.[1]

Pawnee Bill's duties as Oklahoma Boomer did not detain him long. His backers were too near legitimate success to take chances, and kept him under wraps until the legal land rush. Although his publicity made the most of it, Gordon W. Lillie's part in the opening of Oklahoma has had scant notice from Oklahoma historians. Per-

[1]Reynolds, *Pioneer Circuses of the West*, p. 151.

48

Plate IV. Buffalo Bill's Wild West. The Visit of Their Majesties.

This Indian Boy looked at the King and tried to steal his umbrella, according to Colonel Cody in an article on "The Wild West in Europe" in the *Sunday Magazine* of the *Philadelphia Press*, May 12, 1907. Cody identified the five-year-old as Cracking Ice, who had seized the gold-handled and crested umbrella and ran with it. King Edward, says Cody, "chased the tiny culprit under the palms, through passageways, around the tepees, and into a corner where he finally captured Little Cracking Ice — and presented him with the umbrella." Cody was incensed, but Queen Alexandra laughed heartily, and the King "declared he had not enjoyed himself quite so much since he was a youngster in knee breeches." The original painting by Arthur Jule Goodman is in the Buffalo Bill Museum, Cody, Wyoming. The reproduction is from a lithograph poster by Stafford & Company, Netherfield near Nottingham, England — 40 x 29½ inches.
Don Russell Collection

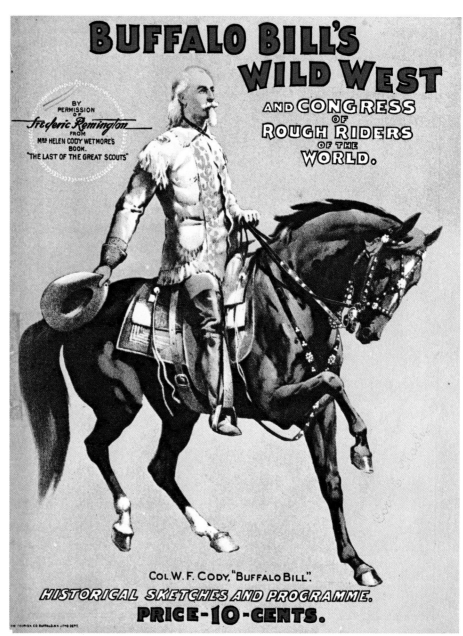

Plate V. Frederic Remington's portrait of Buffalo Bill

Many famous artists contributed to the art of the show poster. This Remington portrait was reproduced in color in a 1909 courier for Buffalo Bill's Wild West and Pawnee Bill's Great Far East. Although credited to Helen Cody Wetmore's *Last of the Great Scouts*, the original of the picture used in the book was in black and white. The lithographer has added color and made other slight changes to conform to poster composition. Color lithograph. 9½ x 8 inches.
Amon Carter Museum Collection.

haps his backers felt guilty over letting him down and backed him in reorganizing his show late in 1889. At all events he was back on the road in 1890, missing only one season.

Did Pawnee Bill's new show resume the title he had used before? A show's correct title cannot always be determined from its advertising. Often it appears several ways in the same publication; for example: Pawnee Bill's Historic (also Historical) Wild West, Mexican Hippodrome, Indian Museum, and — the last phrase appears variously as "Encampment," "Exhibition," and "Grand Fireworks Exhibition."

Pawnee Bill's Historic (or Historical) Wild West held on, with these and other variant billings, and with some ups and downs, until merged with Buffalo Bill at the close of the 1908 season. Through most of this time it was rated among the big shows. One of its assets was Miss May Lillie, "Champion Girl Shot of the West," although a show herald admits she was born in Pennsylvania and brought up in a Quaker community. Gordon W. Lillie and May Manning, a graduate of Smith College, were married August 31, 1886. She took a crash course in Western ways and was given a gold medal for rifle shooting at Philadelphia in 1887 and won the Piedmont Medal at Atlanta, Georgia, in 1889.

Another star, also in the family, was Albert Lillie, younger brother of Gordon, billed as Oklahoma Al, king of the cowboys, rider and roper. He had been foreman of Pawnee Bill's ranch on Medicine River from 1884 to 1886. The show was not long on big names. Only "Iodine, the Trapper" got a full-page billing in an 1893 courier. He was Lewis Vosburg. He claimed to be a survivor of Kit Carson's band, and could "tell many startling and romantic tales to those who visit Pawnee Bill's Historical Wild West." The same courier asserted, "Spotted Tail is with the Historical Wild West," but the great Spotted Tail was killed by Crow Dog at Rosebud Agency in 1881. Perhaps it was Little Spotted Tail, the Brulé chief's son. Young-Man-Afraid-of-His-Horses is mentioned; this also was the junior of that name, but authentically an important figure in the 1890-1891 Sioux War. The most important Indian on the show was Geronimo. He toured at least one season, probably 1906. Others were White Wolf of the Comanches, Stumbling Bear of the Cheyennes, and Left Hand, a veteran of Frank North's Pawnee Scouts. Bright Star was billed as "the handsomest Indian princess

May Manning, later known as the "Champion Girl Shot of the West," and Pawnee Bill (Gordon W. Lillie) were married on August 31, 1886. *Pentz Swords, photographer; courtesy of the Denver Public Library Western Collection.*

in the world." Señorita Rosalia added glamor to the Mexican vaquero events headed by Señor Francisco. José Barrera, famous as Mexican Joe, joined in 1898. Other performers were Trapper Tom; Mustang Walter; Cyclone John Eaton, bronc rider; Horse-Hair George Esler, wild horse rider; Wichita Jim, steer rider; George Hooker, Pony Express rider; and Deadshot Dick Wilbur Collins.

The Mountain Meadows Massacre was an unexpected subject for spectacle in the Pawnee Bill show, which also created an event centered on Wounded Knee and perhaps the Custer fight, frequently featured in billing. A grand artillery race was competition for the chariot races of circuses. An Indian village and a museum were other attractions. In later years a train robbery spectacle was added, but more sensational was the act of Frank L. Sylvis in the part of horse thief. Sylvis was lassoed by José Barrera, thrown from his horse, dragged around the arena at the end of a rope, then convincingly hanged to a pole. Eventually he was cut down to do his act another day.

In 1890 the Pawnee Bill show toured from Montreal to Atlanta, and for the two following years had successful seasons in the Eastern states. By 1893 the aggregation boasted 300 men and women and 200 horses. The route that year included four Canadian provinces. In 1894 King Leopold II invited Lillie to bring his show to the International Industrial and Fine Arts Exhibition at Antwerp, May 5 to October 2, and this time Pawnee Bill made it. After it was over Lillie made the mistake of trying to tour Belgium, only to find that almost everyone in the country had been to the fair. His animals, wagons, and equipment were seized for debt, but he was rescued by a Belgian nobleman, who put up 3,500 francs and suggested the show move to Holland. There it was more successful, particularly after a command performance before Queen Wilhelmina, who seems to have had a weakness for Wild West shows. Lillie refused pay for this, but, when pressed, asked permission to give Sunday performances, which was granted.

After touring France, the Pawnee Bill show returned to the United States, but Lillie was $10,000 in debt because he had to repair his wagons for the following season. The lumberman who had supplied him guaranteed the debt and by the end of the season Lillie was $30,000 in the black. By the end of the 1898 season he had a surplus of $65,000 and invested in the Arkansas Valley

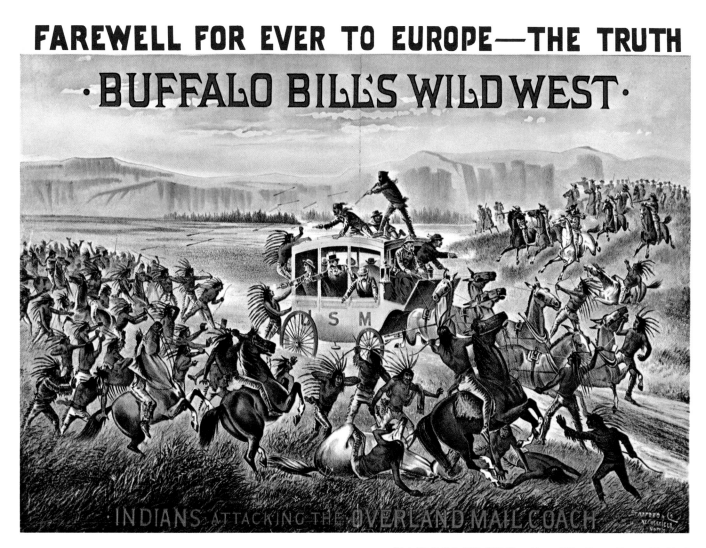

FAREWELL FOR EVER TO EUROPE—THE TRUTH

· BUFFALO BILL'S WILD WEST ·

INDIANS ATTACKING THE OVERLAND MAIL COACH

Plate VI. Buffalo Bill's Wild West: Farewell For Ever to Europe: The Truth

The Indians' attack on the Deadwood Stage Coach was a fixture in Buffalo
Bill programs. Buffalo Bill conducted several tours, and
finally told "the truth" in 1903.
Color lithograph. 30 x 40 inches.
Don Russell Collection.

Bank of Pawnee, Oklahoma. The gravy train was apparently still on the track in 1902 when Pawnee Bill's Historic Wild West Company published J. H. De Wolff's life of Pawnee Bill, *From the Saddle of a Cowboy and Ranger to the Chair of a Bank President.*

Whether the Pawnee Bill show became big time is difficult to determine. It seems to have left little traditional impress. Pawnee Bill is mainly remembered as partner of Buffalo Bill, and it is often necessary to emphasize that his previous show was not called Pawnee Bill's Far East, as was the title in the combination. The Far East idea, however, was Lillie's.

The Wild West show in its first decade had a contemporary interest that began to fade after the turn of the century. Many personalities who were objects of curiosity in Buffalo Bill's early tours were dead; the survivors were no longer in the news. The contest idea of latter-day rodeo had not been developed. The Wild West format lacked variety. There was a temptation to combine it with a circus, or to add circus acts to Wild West pageantry.

Lillie's solution was to restyle his show as Pawnee Bill's Historic Wild West and Great Far East. The Far East part of it included "every type of male and female inhabitant" — Hindu magicians, Singhalese dancers, Madagascar oxen cavalry, Australian bushmen with boomerangs, Boers, Kaffirs, Abyssinians, Zulus, and Hottentots, Chinese and Japanese cavalry, and of course Cossacks, gauchos, and Arabian horsemen. There was also a daily ascension of "the one perfect airship," rivaling that of Santos Dumont, in 1905. Lillie leased four elephants from William P. Hall on February 3, 1906, adding them to his sacred white camels and buffalo from his Oklahoma Buffalo Ranch. The elephants remained with Pawnee Bill to the end of his show. In 1905 they had been with the only show Hall ever put out under his own name. Thereafter Hall became a circus broker at his Lancaster, Missouri, farm, buying, selling, equipping, sponsoring, and repossessing outdoor shows in bewildering variety. He reclaimed his elephants when the Buffalo Bill-Pawnee Bill show was bankrupted in 1913.[2]

Another somewhat evasive background figure in Wild West show-

[2]Fred Pfening III, "William P. Hall," *Missouri Historical Review,* LXII (April, 1968), p. 292. Glenn Shirley, *Pawnee Bill* (Albuquerque: University of New Mexico Press, 1958), pp. 163-169, seems to have omitted the year. *Bandwagon,* VI (January-February, 1962), 23, shows billing and newspaper review of Far East for July 28, 1905.

These two groups presented popular acts in Buffalo Bill's Wild West Show.
The Bedouins (above) are pictured in Vienna, Austria, in 1890. The Aurora Zouaves,
an amateur drill team billed in 1897 as interstate champions for ten years,
were photographed, flanked by Buffalo Bill, left, and Nate Salsbury, right, in
their home town of Aurora, Illinois, in 1898. Bedouins photographed by G. V. D. Lippe.
Courtesy of the Denver Public Library Western Collection.

56

Plate VII. Buffalo Bill's Wild West and Congress of Rough Riders of the World

was presented in 1895 "in the grandest of illuminated arenas:
two electric plants, 250,000 candle power." Sufficient light for night performances
had been a problem since the show's beginnings in 1883,
and although the solution was advertised as "lighter than day," a lighting
system that would permit a night baseball game was still a half century away.
The poster illustrates many features of the show.
Color lithograph. 26 x 78 inches.
Courtesy of the Library of Congress.

manship came into the Pawnee Bill show management at about the time of the Far East concept. This was Edward Arlington, a veteran of the Barnum & Bailey staff. He was active during the 1907 season, but moved on in 1908 when Pawnee Bill decided to spend the entire working year at Wonderland Park, Boston.

Many more Wild West shows sprang up in the 1890's, especially after Buffalo Bill's triumph at the Chicago World's Fair, but many of them left little more trace than a name in the record. One that had reputation as well as name was William Levi Taylor, known as Buck Taylor, King of the Cowboys in Buffalo Bill's Wild West for many years and in a series of dime novels by Prentiss Ingraham, claimed as the first stories with a cowboy hero. Buck Taylor's Wild West flourished, or failed to flourish, in 1894. He retired to a Wyoming ranch and died in Downington, Pennsylvania in 1924.

Stowe & Long's Circus, Menagerie, Wild West and Balloon Shows, 1889, might well have anticipated the Far East idea, and so could Sutton's American Wild West and Roman Hippodrome, 1890. O'Dell's Famous Hippodrome and F. J. McCarthy's Arizona Wild West came along in 1893, as did Kennedy Brothers Wild West, sometimes known as Kennedy's XIT Ranch Show. Kemp Sisters' Wild West is said to have had the first Wild West show ad in *Billboard* when that magazine of the outdoor show world started in 1896 — and while "Brothers" has wide usage in circus nomenclature, a "Sisters" show is a rarity.

58

Buffalo Bill's Wild West reached its peak as a major attraction in the decade 1887 to 1896.
In 1894 the Indians (above) drew crowds to Ambrose Park, South Brooklyn, adjoining the 39th
Street Ferry, where the covered grand stand seated 20,000. The show played before many
of the crowned heads of Europe; at one performance June 20, 1887, four kings, including Leopold II,
King of the Belgians, rode in the Deadwood coach. King Leopold was back June 24 for another
performance and is shown (below at right) as he visited Colonel Cody's headquarters tent.
Those with him may include Crown Prince Baldwin, 18 years old, who died in 1891, and Albert, 12,
who was Belgian king during World War I.
Courtesy of the Denver Public Library Western Collection.

FOURTH EPISODE—
The Passing of a Golden Age

Anyone who can remember the days when a circus arrived in town at dawn, unloaded its wagons from the flat-cars of a train, set up its tents, put on a monster, free street parade followed by afternoon and evening performances, and then stole away in the night to do all of this over again in some other town next day, knows that for weeks after such a visit every small boy and some girls tried to imitate all the acts they had seen. On occasion the town's children would pool their talents, pony carts, bicycles, band instruments, and borrowed finery and put on a circus of their own.

Wild West shows had more sophisticated imitators. By this time many a cowhand had been in and out of a Wild West show. When he got home he showed off his skills at the next roundup, or at the riding and roping contests that became a part of July Fourth celebrations. Of course the Wild West show performers had been recruited from these same informal meets, not yet called rodeos. Denver offered prizes for events at an exposition in 1887, and Buck Taylor, "King of the Cowboys," superintended Denver's Cowboy Tournament and Wild West in 1890. July 4, 1888, was proclaimed Frontier Day in Prescott. But claiming the title of "Daddy of 'em all" is Cheyenne Frontier Days, which has been held continuously since 1897.

The stated purpose of the 1897 Cheyenne Frontier Days was to "revive the thrilling incidents and pictures of life that may be reproduced in form by those who were once actors in that period." If that seems close to the purpose of the original Buffalo Bill's Wild West, so does the program. Of the eight announced contests, six were cowpony, wild horse, and free-for-all races at various distances. The two others were roping and wild bronco riding. There were also feature and spectacle events: a sham battle by troops from Fort D. A. Russell, a simulated hanging by vigilantes, an ox train on the overland trail, a stagecoach holdup, and the inevitable Pony Express ride.[1]

The second Frontier Days in 1898 went the rest of the way. Buffalo Bill's Wild West appeared at the celebration.

Buffalo Bill's Wild West never topped its 1893 success in Chicago. However, it did not hit the skids immediately. The 1894 season was spent in greater New York, mainly in Ambrose Park, South Brooklyn, near the 39th Street ferry. The grandstand had 20,000 seats. Two performances at fifty cents admission meant a sell-out take of $20,000, but expenses were $4,000 a day, and there were many days they did not even make expenses. Cody was in debt at the end of the season. A more serious setback was the illness of Nate Salsbury, who never resumed active management of the show.

Salsbury is represented as the astute businessman who kept the show going while Cody frittered away the profits in gold mines, patent medicines, and other unprofitable investments. That is not the whole story. Salsbury was a director in Cody's company to develop the Big Horn Basin and city of Cody, Wyoming. Salsbury Beach, Long Island, was solely Nate's unprofitable idea. So was the show he put together under the name of Black America. Salsbury, perhaps, was ahead of his time in assuming that the Black South could be dramatized as well as the Wild West. He employed 300 Negro entertainers, traveling in fifteen railway cars. It was a time when minstrel shows were popular — Christy, Primrose, and Al G. Fields. They were done in blackface, but not by Blacks, until the great Bert Williams broke the barrier and went all the way to Broadway's top, the Ziegfeld Follies. Only a few years later Negro spirituals became immensely popular. But Black America proved an immediate and expensive failure.

With Salsbury out of action a deal was made with James A. Bailey, who was to provide transportation and local expenses in exchange for a share in the profits of the Buffalo Bill show.

The name of Barnum is generally considered synonymous with circus, yet P. T. Barnum, who spent most of his life promoting Barnum's Museum, Jenny Lind, Tom Thumb, and other attractions, came late to the outdoor show world and left only moderate impress on it. The junior partner of Barnum & Bailey is by far a greater circus name. It should be; he picked it for the purpose. When

[1]Robert D. Hanesworth, *Daddy of 'Em All: The Story of Cheyenne Frontier Days* (Cheyenne: Flintlock Publishing Company, 1967), pp. 13-30.

orphaned James Anthony McGinness ran away with a circus he attached himself to a press agent claiming descent from Hachaliah Bailey, whose Old Bet is said to have been the first elephant exhibited in America. James A. changed his last name to Bailey, and by age thirty he was successfully engaged in the Cooper & Bailey circus. After a series of mergers involving Barnum, James L. Hutchinson, and W. W. Cole, a show emerged in 1888 with the famed Barnum & Bailey label. Adam Forepaugh died in 1890 and his show was taken over by Barnum & Bailey.

Barnum died in 1891, leaving Bailey in control of the Greatest Show on Earth. After taking control of the Buffalo Bill show in 1895 and combining Forepaugh & Sells Brothers in 1896 as the Biggest Show on Earth, Bailey could route three of the largest outdoor shows in America. He had one serious rival, however. The five Ringling brothers had built a wagon show into the big time in eleven years and were ready to claim a place as the World's Greatest Show.

Bailey sent the Buffalo Bill show over a 9,000-mile route in 1895, to 131 stands in 190 days. The Wild West had never before made so many one-day stops — and was not equipped for it. For twelve years it had played long runs at expositions or big cities with only occasional tours. Bailey's strategy paid off in taking Colonel Cody and his show to localities where they had not been seen before. In 1896 the show traveled 10,000 miles to 132 stands; in 1897 it played Madison Square Garden in New York and went on to 103 other cities.

There were few changes in the show in these years. A successful program had been found and they stayed with it. In 1894 South American gauchos were advertised as making their first appearance in the United States. Riffian Arabian horsemen joined the Congress of Rough Riders of the World. A Zouave infantry drill by the celebrated Aurora Zouaves, ten years interstate champions, also derived from North Africa by way of France and Colonel Elmer E. Ellsworth's Zouaves of the Civil War period. The Zouave drill was spectacular, done in a double-time half-step with the men touching elbows in a sequence of wheelings and patterns directed by whistle signals. The climax was wall scaling in which the Zouaves formed a human pyramid, the last man being hoisted to the top with the aid of rifles and rifle-slings.

It was a period when military drill had a popular following, when private armies, armed with swords only, were maintained by Knights of Pythias, Knights Templar, Knights of Columbus, Knights and Ladies of Honor, and many other lodges. Buffalo Bill's Wild West presented infantry drill, cavalry drill, and artillery drill. The Spanish-American War stimulated further military display. A color guard of Cuban War veterans appeared in the 1898 program.

The most publicized unit in the war was Roosevelt's Rough Riders, formally the First United States Volunteer Cavalry commanded by Colonel Leonard Wood; Theodore Roosevelt was lieutenant colonel. The show publicity immediately tied Teddy's corps to the Rough Riders of the World. In 1899 sixteen veterans of Roosevelt's Rough Riders joined those of the Wild West giving the claim validity, and a spectacle of the "Battle of San Juan Hill" replaced "Custer's Last Fight." A few Cubans, Filipinos, and Hawaiians in the pageant represented our new islands and their people.

The Wild West was being updated almost too rapidly. In 1901 and 1902 the spectacle was changed to "The Allied Powers at the Battle of Tien-Tsin and the Capture of Pekin," a re-enactment of events of the Boxer Rebellion in China of 1900. As an international force was used it gave the Buffalo Bill show opportunity to employ all its military Rough Riders. Another military feature was a Gatling gun drill. The Gatling gun, a machine gun with multiple barrels that fired in succession, was invented in 1862, but won acclaim at Santiago under Captain James Parker. Its principle was rediscovered during World War II. The drill was spectacular. The gun was mounted on a light artillery carriage; wheels were exchanged between gun and carriage by manpower with bewildering speed; and the rapid fire of blank ammunition was noisy and satisfying.

Cody was invited to accompany General Nelson Miles to the front in 1898, but Miles himself was delayed in getting into action, and Cody, although he went so far as to send his horses Knickerbocker and Lancer ahead for use in Puerto Rico, was not able to break away from his show in mid-season. There was some compensation, however, in what a program proclaims as "the crowning day in Colonel Cody's life," Cody Day at the Omaha Trans-Mississippi Exposition, August 31, 1898. Fifteen years had passed since Cody had launched the Wild West in Omaha, and this was homecoming. Alexander Majors was there, representing Russell Majors & Waddell, the company that employed Cody on its famous Pony Express. Edward Creighton, who had built the first telegraph line across the Plains,

Aurora Zouaves Scaling a Wall. This amateur drill team, organized by Captain G. Al Hurd in Aurora, Illinois, in 1887, was billed as ten years interstate champion when it joined the Buffalo Bill's Wild West in 1897. Their costume, imitative of a French North Africa tribe, included white leggings, baggy red trousers, dark blue coat, light blue vest, yellow sash, and tasseled red fez.

Captain Albert H. Tarble, who headed the Zouaves for fifty years, directed their intricate tight-order drill, done at double time and climaxed by the entire company going over a wall, aided only by their rifles, with which they improvised ladders, or pulled each other up, even to the last man.

Courtesy of the Aurora Historical Museum, Aurora, Illinois.

putting the Pony Express out of business, also was there. Cody was hailed by Governor Silas A. Holcomb and Senator John M. Thurston.

Buffalo Bill's Wild West was only briefly an attraction at Omaha. However, a competent observer listed the three great features of the Trans-Mississippi as "the food exhibit, the electrical exhibit and — the Indians." Octave Thanet (real name Alice French), whose *The Man of the Hour* has been hailed as a start toward realism in fiction and whose *Stories of a Western Town* attests she was no tenderfoot, insisted that the Indian Congress was "not a Wild West show, but a serious ethnological exhibition."[2] However, serious competition for Buffalo Bill's Wild West was developing.

The Indian Congress was managed by Colonel Frederic T. Cummins. Born in 1859 at Council Bluffs where his father Hiram was an Indian trader, Fred grew up among Indians, was a trader, prospector, cowboy, and bronco breaker in such places as Deadwood, Helena, the Coeur d'Alene country, and Standing Rock Agency. His publicity biography tells of some encounters with Indians and highwaymen that are not so extravagant as to be entirely unbelieveable. It does not explain how his military title was attained.[3]

Whatever his background — and apparently it did not include show business at this time — Cummins had the full backing of the Indian Bureau. Geronimo and the other Apache prisoners of war were brought from Fort Sill to Omaha for the Indian Congress. In all, thirty-one tribes were represented. Collectors remember the Omaha fair for the many Indian portraits photographed by F. A. Rinehart. Renamed the Greater American Exposition, the fair continued through 1899 with the Indian Congress featured. Cummins then went to work to put together an even greater Indian Congress for the Pan-American Exposition in Buffalo in 1901. There forty-two tribes were represented. Red Cloud, Oglala Sioux chief in the war of 1868, sometimes called Red Cloud's War and including the Fetterman massacre and the siege of Fort Phil Kearny, appeared at Buffalo. Cummins' Indian Congress toured New England through 1902 and appeared at Madison Square Garden in 1903, where Chief Joseph of the Nez Percé was star attraction. After the New York engagement Cummins spent the rest of the year getting ready for an even greater Indian Congress —

[2]Octave Thanet [Alice French], "The Trans-Mississippi Exposition," *Cosmopolitan*, XXV (October, 1898), 599-614.

[3]Richmond C. Hill, *A Great White Indian Chief . . . Col. Fred Cummins*, Young Buffalo Wild West and Col. Fred Cummins' Far East Combined, 1912.

fifty-one tribes this time — at the Louisiana Purchase Exposition in St. Louis in 1904. He hit the road again in 1905 and 1906, by this time backing off from the serious ethnological exhibition and adding Wild West to the title as well as more than a trace of circus. When Cummins' Wild West played Pittsfield, Massachusetts, June 1, 1906, the show had four elephants, one camel, seven cages of wild animals, and three tableau wagons. It was as Cummins' Wild West and Indian Congress that the show toured Europe from 1907 to 1911, including Great Britain, Belgium, Germany, Switzerland, France, and Italy.[4]

With Red Cloud, Chief Joseph, and Geronimo appearing at various times in his cast of characters, Cummins rivaled Cody in presenting Indians of historic importance — and Cummins also billed such Cody veterans as Red Shirt, American Horse, Conquering Bear, Flat Iron, and Jack Red Cloud. Cody perhaps had an edge in boasting Sitting Bull (for one season) and the prisoners of war from the last Sioux uprising.

Another Indian of considerable notoriety who made a brief appearance in show business was Rain-in-the-Face. To set the record straight, it is officially documented that he appeared in a show called Sitting Bull's Log Cabin, conducted by P. B. Wickham of Mandan, North Dakota, in the Midway Plaisance of the Chicago World's Fair of 1893. The cabin was the one in which Sitting Bull was killed, and the Indian Bureau inspector reported that the nine Indians with the show were "all genuine Sioux. Rain-in-the-Face, celebrated by Longfellow and reputed by some to have killed Custer, is here, though he consistently makes no pretensions in the matter. . . ." The inspector also paid his dubious respects to the nearby American Indian Village of sixty Indians in charge of "Buckskin Joe," Henry De Ford of Topeka, Kansas. "The performers . . . exhibit the quondam degradation of the tribes. The explanations and historical information given by Buckskin Joe are of the most meager character, and this show is a failure and a disgrace."[5] This, of course, was not the "Buckskin Joe" (Edward Jonathan Hoyt) of Buckskin Joe's Wild West.

The Office of Indian Affairs, it might be mentioned, authorized only two shows to exhibit Indians in 1893, those of Buffalo Bill and Pawnee

[4]"Cummins' Wild West Show," *Bandwagon*, VI (July-August, 1962), 4.
[5]Daniel Dorchester, "62nd Annual Report of the Commissioner of Indian Affairs," in U. S. Congress, *House Executive Documents*, No. 1, Pt. 5, 53rd Cong., 2nd Sess., p. 395.

Wild West show performers many times found that the "spectacles" were too real. They could not get too close to the burning wagon (above) without suffering injury from smoke or fire.
The view of the Young Buffalo Wild West Show grounds (below) gives a very good picture of arena (on the right) and the back lot.
Courtesy of the Circus World Museum, Baraboo, Wisconsin.

Bill. Cody and Salsbury took 100 and were required

> to pay the Indians for their services a fair compensation, to furnish them proper food and clothing, to pay their traveling and needful incidental expenses from the date of leaving the agencies until their return thereto, to protect them from all immoral influences and surroundings, to provide all needful medical attendance and medicine, to do everything that may be requisite for their health, comfort, and welfare, and to return the Indians to their reservations within the time specified by the Interior Department without charge or cost to them.

To insure this responsibility, Cody and Salsbury were put under $10,000 bond. The same terms and conditions were required of Pawnee Bill, but his bond was fixed at $5,000. Possibly he had half as many Indians.[6]

Another notorious Western character that Cummins show publicity claimed as "never connected with any other public exhibition" was Calamity Jane, one of whose real names was Martha Jane Canary. However, Calamity Jane's pamphlet autobiography, in which she tells so little about herself that is factual, was written for Kohl and Middleton's Palace Museum in Minneapolis, where she appeared in 1896. She is said to have sold some of the pamphlets at Cummins' Indian Congress at the Pan-American Exposition.

Top billing for notorious characters, however, goes to the Cole Younger and Frank James Wild West of 1903. The surviving Younger brother had been paroled in 1901 after the bandit gang had come to grief in attempting to rob a bank in Northfield, Minnesota. The James boys escaped from Northfield; Jesse was killed in 1882, and Frank surrendered to Governor T. T. Crittenden. He was tried on several charges and acquitted because of insufficient evidence. Remaining charges were nol prossed. Chicago showmen financed the production; its headliners attracted gamblers and grifters from far and near. Actually the ex-bandits were trying to go straight and Frank James advised police chiefs on the route ahead of the character of the show. But, "The show is without exception the poorest ever seen in our city," declared a Maryville, Missouri, newspaper of August 29, 1903. A few names have been recorded: John Gill, band leader; R. H. Dockrill, equestrian director; Lew Nichols, side-show manager; Howard Damon, purchasing agent; and James Whalen, boss canvasman. It had a short life.[7]

[6]Dorchester, "62nd Annual Report," p. 59.
[7]Homer Croy, *Jesse James Was My Neighbor* (New York: Duell, Sloan, and Pearce, 1949), pp. 212-214, tells more about it than other Jesse James and Younger brothers books, including the quote. Croy says the show returned to Maryville in 1908, but most authorities give it only one season.

While the largest number of outdoor shows is claimed for 1885, and the biggest Wild West show success was that of Buffalo Bill in 1893, it seems evident that the largest number of Wild West shows flourished in the early years of the twentieth century. Many of them were small, designed to play county fairs and carnivals, and could be produced with limited capital. Whereas even the smallest of circuses required at least one elephant, a lion or two, a band wagon, and a calliope, a Wild West show could get by with a stagecoach and a covered wagon. In these decades stagecoaches were making their last stands in short-haul lines in the West; many were being abandoned and could be bought cheap. A covered wagon could be any farm wagon, as in fact were many of those driven by pioneers in crossing the Plains. And a farm wagon was not yet an antique, even in 1920. Range horses could be picked up at $5 to $20, and the more they bucked the better. Barbed wire fences ended the long drives and the big roundups, so many cowboys were seeking other employment. Roustabouts could be hired even cheaper. Anyone with a goatee and mustache vaguely resembling Buffalo Bill could be the star.

The St. Louis World's Fair seemed to have unusually stimulated outdoor show business. Cummins took off from there for a tour under canvas. Carl Hagenbeck's wild animals were there, toured for two seasons, and then joined Benjamin E. Wallace in the famous Wallace & Hagenbeck circus. A Boer War spectacle at the Fair toured for one season. (By supplying horses for the Boer War, William P. Hall started his circus supply farm at Lancaster, Missouri.) And at Delmar Garden outside the exposition grounds that summer was Gabriel Brothers Champion Long Distance Riders Wild West. Jim and Kid Gabriel had ridden in Buffalo Bill's Cowboy Race from Chadron, Nebraska, to the World's Fair in Chicago in 1893, but did not finish so their titular claim was a thin one.

The Gabriel brothers had a run-in with Charles H. Tompkins in 1903 on the Great Forepaugh Wild West Shows, also known as the Fish-Luella Forepaugh Wild West, mainly of interest because it indicates that this show was staging Adam Forepaugh's spectacle of "Custer's Last Fight" — which Tompkins also was to stage in his own show, 1911-1914. Luella was Adam Forepaugh's daughter. Fish was her husband; possibly Charles W. Fish and probably the Charles Fish who was a famous bareback horseman.[8]

[8]Charles H. Tompkins, "Gabriel Brothers Wild West," *The Westerners Brand Book*, [Chicago] XIII (October, 1956), 64.

Buffalo Bill at the Indian Congress. This photograph probably was taken at Colonel Fred Cummins Indian Congress at the Pan-American Exposition, Buffalo, 1901, where many prominent Indians were assembled. Identified are: left to right, Rain-in-the-Face, Red Shirt, Crazy Head, Red Cloud, Buffalo Bill, Chief Gall, American Horse, Crow King, and Spotted Tail. Cummins publicity names Red Shirt, American Horse, and Red Cloud, but the youthful appearance suggests Jack Red Cloud, son of the famed chief and veteran of Buffalo Bill's Wild West, as were Red Shirt and American Horse, and possibly Gall. The famous Spotted Tail was killed in 1881, so this may be Young Spotted Tail, who never attained his father's prominence. Rain-in-the-Face is not known to have been in any Wild West show, but was on occasion in minor show business.
Courtesy of the Denver Public Library Western Collection.

While none of these shows had valid claim to being the Greatest (Wild West) Show on Earth, undoubtedly some of them so advertised themselves. At the other end of the scale, the smallest Wild West show ever to take the road was without question that of Buckskin Ben. Chief William Red Fox, veteran performer with Buffalo Bill, Miller Brothers, and other shows, related that he saw Buckskin Ben's Wild West on the courthouse square at Terre Haute, Indiana. Ben came out of Cambridge, Indiana, with one horse, one ring, and sufficient tentage to cover them and a quickie audience. His Little Top did not crowd the courthouse lawn. Ben's wife beat the drum and sold tickets at the same time — and never missed a beat.

A number of other shows flourished during the first decade of the twentieth century,[9] but Buffalo Bill's Wild West was still the unrivaled big one as it completed eight years of barnstorming the United States in 1902. There had been setbacks. As the show left Charlotte, North Carolina, October 28, 1901, for Danville, Virginia, its last stop of the season, its second section had a head-on collision with a freight train. No one was killed, but Annie Oakley suffered serious injuries and was out of show business for more than a year. She had fired her last shot for Buffalo Bill. In the wreck 110 horses were killed, including Cody's Old Pap.

At the end of a coast-to-coast tour in 1902, the show returned to London to begin what was to prove its last European tour. On Christmas eve Nate Salsbury died; the show opened two days later, on Boxing Day, with flags at half staff. It was a heavy blow for Cody, who possibly had been trying to get out of show business all the time he was in it. He sought prosperity in ranching in Nebraska, in a gold mine in Arizona, in a patent medicine with White Beaver (Dr. David

[9]Broncho John, Famous Western Horseman, and His Corps of Expert Horsemen (J. H. Sullivan), 1906; Buckskin Ben's Wild West and Dog and Pony Show (Benjamin Stalker), 1908-1913; Buckskin Bill's Wild West, about 1900; Buffalo and Wild West, 1902; Carlisle's Wild West (R. C. Carlisle), about 1909; Cherokee Ed's Wild West (Ed Baumeister) 1909 only, failed in midseason; Dickey's Circle D Ranch, 1909 (combined as Circle D Ranch Wild West & Cooper Brothers Famous Shows, 1914); Diamond Bar Ranch Wild West, 1909; Indian Bill's Wild West (J. A. Jones), 1903, became Indian Bill's Wild West and Cole & Rogers Circus Combined, 1906, probably the Jones Brothers Buffalo Ranch Wild West, 1910, and Kit Carson's Buffalo Ranch Wild West (Thomas F. Wiedemann) 1911; Lone Star May's Wild West, 1909; Captain Ed Senechal's Wild West (had twenty buffaloes) 1904; Snyder Brothers Wild West, 1909; Texas Bill's Wild West, about 1904, became Yankee Robinson Three-Ring Circus and Texas Bill's Wild West (Fred Buchanan) 1911-1912; Texas Bud's Wild West (P. J. Snell), 1909; and Tiger Bill's Wild West (Dave W. Perrine), 1909-1913; one report puts it as early as 1902; taken over by Emmett D. Snyder, about 1914-1934.

Franklin Powell), in a colonization project in Mexico with Lieutenant Frederick Schwatka, and in the development of Cody, Wyoming (Cody had dedicated the Irma Hotel, named for his daughter, in November before leaving for London). None of these investments paid off, but a lot of profits from the show went into them. The one-day stands were wearing Cody out, and he was ready to quit, but was too heavily in debt.

Bailey's strategy in handling the Buffalo Bill show was to trade territory with the Barnum & Bailey Circus, which toured Europe from 1897 to 1902. They swapped railway cars and equipment — an immediately practical consideration. Bailey's other show, Forepaugh & Sells Brothers, had been holding the fort at home, or trying to, but Ringling Brothers were coming up fast, and Bailey made a deal with them, cutting them in on Forepaugh management and routing. It has been said that Bailey kept Buffalo Bill in Europe for four seasons to keep it out of competition with his shows in the United States. However, it would seem quite logical that he should consider the Wild West a better bet for European interest, and it had been a decade since Buffalo Bill had been seen abroad. There can be no doubt that the Buffalo Bill show sparked an immense interest in the American West for Europeans, an interest that continues to this day, although this last tour ended in 1906.

King Edward VII, who as Prince of Wales had been a booster for the show on previous visits, was disappointingly absent this time, waiting until March 14, 1903, three weeks before the show left London, to appear. However, he visited the backlot where an Indian boy grabbed for his umbrella, an episode that was subject of a painting by Arthur Jule Goodman used in posters and other show advertising. During this tour the future King George V and the future King Edward VIII (later Duke of Windsor) saw the show, making four successive crowned heads of England who were patrons of Buffalo Bill's Wild West.

A tour of English cities started April 13 at Manchester and continued, despite rain and storms in October, until October 23 at Burton-on-Trent. Winter quarters were at Stoke-on-Trent. The 1904 season, which included Wales, Cornwall, and Scotland, was very prosperous, especially in Glasgow and Edinburgh. Again they wintered at Stoke-on-Trent at the heavy cost of $150,000.

The engagement in Paris, April 2 to June 4, 1905, was called the most prosperous in tent-show history. It also rated the largest program printed for Buffalo Bill's Wild West, eighty pages, mostly given to a heavily illustrated life of Cody. The twenty-four events were largely the traditional — "Custer's Last Stand" spectacle, attack on an emigrant train, the Deadwood stagecoach, Pony Express, drill by cavalry and artillery, Rough Riders, and races and shooting; "cowboy fun" became in French, *"cowboys dans leurs divertissements"*, but not yet the Spanish *rodeo*. Johnny Baker was shooting headliner; Joe Esquivel was chief of cowboys, and Vincent Orapeza, champion roper, was chief of the vaqueros. Heading the Indians was the famous Iron Tail, called the Indian on the buffalo nickel. (James Earle Fraser, the designer, once wrote, "I used three different heads; I remember two of the men: Iron Tail, the best Indian head I can remember; the other was Two Moons, the third I cannot recall. . . .")[10]

Other chiefs named in the program were Hard Whip, Cheyennes; Comes First, Oglalas; Black Heart, Arapahos; Blue Shield, Brulé; and Lone Bear of the Indian police. Luther Standing Bear, interpreter in England in 1902, reveals a bit of fakery here. His seventy-five Indians were all Sioux, but were divided into tribes for the Grand Review according to the color of their horses — and Sioux were playing the parts of Cheyenne and Arapaho.

This is one of a very few programs with mention of a side-show — or *Annexe* in Paris, with an admission charge of fifty centimes (translation: 9.65 cents, or a thin dime) — another concession to circus ideas. The *Annexe* was traditional: snake charmer, dwarf, giant, sword swallower, magicians, contortionists, trained birds, and monkeys.

The one-day and two-day stands after Paris were at places much more familiarly known two world wars later — Chartres, Alencon, Fleurs, St. Lo, Cherbourg, Rouen, Le Havre, Arras, Donar, Calais, Boulogne, then Lille for four days. Bailey visited the show for the last time July 4 at Lille. The tour continued: Reims, Charleville, Sedan, Verdun, Luneville, Belfort, Lyons. The Shah of Persia saw the show at Vichy. The season closed after a stand in Marseille from November 1 to 12.

The show had competition in France that summer from McCaddon's International Shows and Wild West. Buffalo Bill won and the

[10]*The Wi-Iyohi*, VII (June, 1953).

The Miller brothers, George, Zack, and Joe, guided the fortunes of the 101 Ranch Wild West Show.

Courtesy of the Oklahoma Historical Society.

"The first cowgirl," Lucille Mulhall, was present when the 101 Ranch performers entertained the National Editorial Association June 11, 1905.

Courtesy of the Oklahoma Historical Society.

opposition show was sold out August 17 and its owner, J. T. McCaddon, fled to England to escape creditors. The following year Joseph T. McCaddon, presumably the same, turned up as one of the Bailey heirs, brother of Mrs. Bailey.[11]

A worse trouble was an outbreak of glanders among the horses, first noticed July 10. By the end of the season 200 of the show's 300 horses had been destroyed. Jake Posey, boss hostler, told of taking twelve horses a day; for many days, to an incinerator near Marseille, where they were killed and the bodies burned. (This is the Jake Posey who drove a forty-horse hitch of Percherons drawing the Barnum & Bailey bandwagon in parades. He and his predecessor Jim Thomas were possibly the only drivers of that many horses drawing a wagon.)[12]

James A. Bailey died March 22, 1906. Among his effects was a note for $12,000 signed by Cody. Cody said he had paid it, but there was no proof. The upshot was that Cody owned a heavily-mortgaged one-third of the show, and the Bailey heirs already had taken over the Salsbury interest. They were Mrs. Ruth L. Bailey, her brother Joseph T. McCaddon, W. W. Cole, a famous circus man long associated with Barnum & Bailey, and Albert A. Stewart of the Stewart Lithographing Company.

The show opened in Marseille before Bailey's death, and had a big opening week. It moved by way of Nice into Italy, then entered the Austro-Hungarian Empire at Trieste. Vienna was good for three weeks and after a stop at Budapest there was a month of one-day stands in Hungary. In April Cody felt sufficiently prosperous to donate $5,000 to aid victims of a Mount Vesuvius eruption and $1,000 to San Francisco earthquake and fire relief, but a brief foray across the Russian border was disappointing financially. August business was good in Germany, and after a few stops in Belgium the show closed the season at Arles, France, October 30, 1906.

Cody had to put his show together with very little help for its first American tour in five years. He returned to first principles; the spectacle was the "Battle of Summit Springs," in which he had participated. A motion picture of it has survived and it was a reasonably

[11]Chindahl, *History of the Circus*, p. 257; Stella Adelyne Foote (ed.), *Letters from Buffalo Bill* (Billings, Montana: Foote Publishing Company, 1954), p. 65; Russell, *Lives and Legends of Buffalo Bill*, pp. 443, 445.
[12]Jake Posey, "With Buffalo Bill in Europe," *Bandwagon*, (October, 1953), 4-6; May, *From Rome to Ringling*, pp. 216-223.

accurate reproduction. A new scene was "The Great Train Hold-up and Bandit Hunters of the Union Pacific." The early-day locomotive was built on a motor car, which was in its pioneer stage. An advertisement in the 1907 program gave assurance that "It's safe to buy a Studebaker" and mentioned "our fully equipped garage, situated in the heart of" New York City. Such effects as black smoke puffing from the locomotive and an electric headlight were devised by Miller Reese Hutchinson of the Universal Motor Car Company of New York. The tour opened at Madison Square Garden and stayed on the road for two years, mostly numerous one-day stands. The Bailey Estate was anxious to unload the property and sounded out Gordon W. Lillie on a merger. When Lillie suggested it to Cody in June, 1908, Cody demurred at including Pawnee Bill in the show's title. However, the discussion was friendly; Lillie's suggestions about routing the show proved out, and Cody, after a drag-out fight with Louis E. Cooke, general manager for the Bailey heirs, looked more favorably on the merger idea. The deal was a complicated one, with Cody's remaining financial interest in the show somewhat problematical, but the result for the season of 1909 was Buffalo Bill's Wild West Combined with Pawnee Bill's Great Far East, affectionately shortened by its personnel to the "Two Bills Show" and remembered by them as a happy show.

In the program the Great Far East had a far less important place than in the billing; it was the seventh episode in a total of fourteen. It presented "A Dream of the Orient," and "An Ethnological Congress of Strange Tribes, Clans, Races, and Nations of Peculiar People," including Bedouin Arabs, Whirling Dervishes, Singhalese and Russian dancers, Australian boomerang throwers, a Hindu fakir, South Sea natives, Japanese, Dahomeans, Soudanese, Moors, Persians, Musselmen, and Syrians. All this with a camel caravan and Rossi's Musical Elephants made it very like a circus.

"Football on Horseback . . . seen with this exhibition for the first time in any arena" was played with a five-foot ball and proved a feature long popular in Wild West shows. Retained were the "Battle of Summit Springs," the "Great Train Hold-up," Devlin's Zouaves, artillery drill, and other long-familiar acts. From the Pawnee Bill show came Mexican Joe, featured as illustrating the use of the lasso. He was José Barrera of San Antonio, who had been with Pawnee Bill since 1898. Also featured was Ray Thompson who had manége trained range horses from Texas for circus-type exhibition.

Added in 1910 or 1911 was Rhoda Royal showing twenty high school horses — horses trained in the steps of the Spanish riding school; in general an act in which a horse responded to almost unnoticed signals by his rider through a sequence of fancy steps. His was a name that popped in and out of show business over many years. Rhoda Royal is said to have originated the Wild West after-show concert. In 1900 he leased cars and property of the Walter L. Main Circus and produced The Great Rhoda Royal Australian Railroad Shows — "First Appearance in the United States" — and in it featured Captain Walter C. Sharp's Troop of Rough Riders. This show went broke in 1901 and Main repossessed his equipment. Royal went back to his horse act, sometimes for Main, and worked elephants. From 1919 to 1922 he ran a combination show under variant names: Rhoda Royal Trained Wild Animal and Old Buffalo Wild West, Rhoda Royal World-toured Shows and Old Buffalo Wild West, Rhoda Royal Three Ring Circus combined with Oklahoma Ranch Wild West. The show died April 7, 1922.[13]

Oklahoma Ranch Wild West was a title used in 1913 by Arlington & Beckman — Edward Arlington and Fred Beckman. This was the Edward Arlington who had been with the Pawnee Bill show in 1907. He was also the Arlington of Miller Bros. & Arlington 101 Ranch Real Wild West, which became one of the biggest.

This show started as one of many by-products of an Oklahoma ranch empire founded by George W. Miller in 1892. He had been using the 101 brand since 1881, so the legend that it signified a ranch of 101,000 acres is not in accord with the facts, although the ranch eventually reached 110,000 acres or 172 square miles. After the death of George W. Miller, in 1903, the ranch was run as a family partnership by his three sons Joseph C. Miller, Zack T. Miller, and George L. Miller, who built it into a self-sufficient ranch empire. They set up their own slaughter house, packing plant, and dairy, then a tannery for the hides, and a harness and saddle shop to work the tanned leather. They went in for fruit orchards and established a cannery. After they struck oil on the property, a refinery and a filling station were built. For the benefit of their many employees, a laundry was set up. A company store was essential, and there was a trading post

[13]Joseph T. Bradbury, "The Rhoda Royal Circus, 1919-1922," *Bandwagon*, V (May-June, 1961), 3-19.

These three boys found the 101 Ranch Wild West Show couriers exciting reading. 1930.
Vince Dillon, photographer; courtesy of the Western History Collections,
University of Oklahoma Library.

for their Ponca Indian neighbors.[14]

The National Editorial Association was invited to the 101 Ranch June 11, 1905, for a roundup. Geronimo was the featured attraction, brought from Fort Sill where he was prisoner of war, for his last buffalo hunt — he was to kill a buffalo bought from Charles Goodnight to provide a barbecue.

Some 64,000 spectators came to Salt Fork to see the show the Millers put on without going out of the neighborhood for talent. With editors as the guests of honor the affair was well publicized. But it was not yet show business. Other — but smaller — parties were entertained in a manner later known as dude ranching, and in slack times cowboys from the 101 took part in local events that later would be called rodeo. A bronc-busting exhibition at Enid, Oklahoma, in 1906 was seen by Lewis Schauss, manager of Kansas City's Convention Hall, and he invited the cowboys to put on their act, for pay, at the November horse show. There Rex and Cathcart, promoters planning a midway called the War Path for the Jamestown Tercentenary Exposition in 1907, proposed that the Millers put on a 100-day show there. Schauss got into the act by setting up an engagement at the Chicago Coliseum on the way. Favorable reports from Chicago interested New York promoters, so the 101 Ranch put together a second company to play Brighton Beach, New York.

It is improbable that Miller brothers got into show business entirely by accident, as this sequence of events suggests, for there was a suspiciously large lot of top talent waiting at the 101 for all this lightning to strike. In 1905 Zack Miller went to Fort Worth to hire Bill Pickett, who had made a considerable reputation with a new act he had invented called bulldogging. Bill Pickett was a Negro, perhaps part Indian, born about 1863 in Williamson County, Texas, near Taylor. He became a brush country cowboy. One day in 1903 to save his horse from being gored, Bill leaped for the horns and wrestled the steer to the ground, biting the steer's upper lip in a bulldog grip. It worked so well he tried it again while working for Lee Moore who ran cattle near Rockdale. Moore was impressed with the act and took Pickett to various events around the country to demonstrate his new-found skill. Later Dave McClure took over and billed Pickett

[14]Ellsworth Collings in collaboration with Alma Miller England, *The 101 Ranch* (Norman: University of Oklahoma Press, 1938), pp. 15-17, 25-26, for the brand, pp. 112-126, for the 101 industries; Fred Gipson, *Fabulous Empire: Colonel Zack Miller's Story* (Boston: Houghton Mifflin Company, 1946), passim.

as "The Dusky Demon." Zack Miller wanted the act for the editors' meeting, and Bill Pickett was 101 Ranch star the rest of his days.[15]

Also at that 1905 gathering was Lucille Mulhall, called the "first Cowgirl" by no less authority than Will Rogers. The word "cowgirl" is said to have been coined for her. She was world's lady champion in roping and tying wild steers and broke world records in competition with men. She was born in 1885 in St. Louis. Her father, Zack Mulhall, had been driving cattle and made the 1889 Oklahoma run, establishing a ranch in what became Logan County. At age ten Lucille was a top hand. Her brother Charley became champion; her sisters Agnes (Bossie) and Georgia were riders and ropers, so Colonel Zack Mulhall's Wild West was a family show. It started in St. Louis in 1899 when the Colonel hired the First Regiment Band, attired the players as cowboys, and put on a roping and riding contest. Mulhall's show was ranch-based, entering teams at carnivals, fairs, contests and special events rather than a traveling show. In 1900 a Cowboy Tournament was staged at the Rough Riders reunion in Oklahoma City. Theodore Roosevelt, who had raised the famous Spanish-American War regiment and was a candidate for Vice-President with William McKinley, applauded the fourteen-year-old cowgirl and gave a dinner for the Mulhall sisters. The *New York World*, July 7, 1900, reported:

> Little Miss Mulhall, who weighs only 90 pounds, can break a bronco, lasso and brand a steer and shoot a coyote at 500 yards. She can also play Chopin, quote Browning, construe Vergil, and make mayonnaise dressing. She is a little ashamed of these latter accomplishments, which are a concession to the civilized prejudices of her mother.

In an advertisement for "Cowboys and Indians" at a Confederate Veterans' Reunion the Memphis *Commercial Appeal*, May 29, 1901, announced that "Miss Lucille Mulhall, the daring broncho rider, will appear daily and rope the wildest Texas steers." Will Rogers also took part, but was barely mentioned, in the "grand roping contests, Indian parades, and war dances." The Mulhall troupe appeared at the Des Moines horse show in 1901, at the Cattlemen's Convention in

[15]Dates and facts on Pickett are hazy, but those used seem most reasonable. See Esse Forrester O'Brien, *The First Bulldogger* (San Antonio: Naylor Company, 1961), admitted to be part fiction; Milt Hinkle, "The Dusky Demon," *True West*, VIII (August, 1961), 30-31, 55-59, and also in Hinkle's pamphlet collection, *Old West* (Lakeland, Florida: n. p., n. d.); Glenn D. Shirley, "Bill Pickett, the Man Who Developed Bulldogging," *Golden West*, I (November, 1964); Bill Burchardt, "A Rider of the 101," *Oklahoma Today*, XVIII (Autumn, 1967); and the works cited by Collings, Gipson, and Foghorn Clancy, *My Fifty Years in Rodeo* (San Antonio: Naylor Company, 1952).

Fort Worth in 1903, and at the St. Louis World's Fair of 1904. In 1905 Mulhall took his "cowboy act" to the Madison Square Garden Horse Fair. It was there April 27 that a steer Lucille Mulhall was to rope jumped the fence, scattered the band, and ran into the audience. Tom Mix threw a rope and missed; Will Rogers made the catch and got a mention in the *New York Herald* — his first in a big city newspaper. Although three big names figured in this episode, its importance in their careers has been exaggerated by some chroniclers.

Lucille Mulhall also appeared at the editors' meeting at 101 Ranch that year, and is reported to have ridden for Miller Brothers at the Jamestown Exposition. The Mulhalls played their act on the vaudeville stage for several years and returned to outdoor show business in 1910. Tom Mix, Jim Gabriel, and Ellison Carroll were with them. Their tours ended in 1915. In 1916 Lucille Mulhall had featured billing in the Buffalo Bill and 101 Ranch Wild West Combined.[16]

Will Rogers once said that his show career started with the Mulhalls in 1899. In 1903 he toured South Africa with Texas Jack's Wild West Circus, billed as "The Cherokee Kid," making his way home by touring with Wirth Brothers' Circus in Australia and New Zealand, and then appearing in the Cummins show at the St. Louis World's Fair. After the Madison Square Garden appearance Will went into vaudeville, graduating into the stage and motion pictures.[17]

Miller Brothers competed successfully at Jamestown with spectacles of the *"Monitor* and *Merrimack,"* "Pocahontas and Captain John Smith," "Colonel Francis Ferrari's Trained Wild Animals," and the "Streets of Cairo." Although they found "it was not proving the success of other world fairs," they were encouraged by showings at Richmond, the Georgia State Fair at Atlanta, and Louisville before returning in November to Bliss (later Marland), Oklahoma. By February, 1908, they had decided to make the 101 Ranch Wild West Show a permanent institution and to move into railroad cars for a tour of the country. As they had made no secret of having a second company

[16]"Lucille Mulhall Carried Feminist Banner into the Cattle Country," *Kansas City Star,* January 11, 1941, signed "L. M."; Louise Cheney, "Lucile [*sic*] Mulhall, Fabulous Cowgirl," *Real West,* XII (March, 1969), 13-15, 58-59, 73; Mildred Mulhall Acton, "Lucille Mulhall — The Original Cowgirl," *The Ranchman,* I (February, 1942), 6-7.
[17]Homer Croy, *Our Will Rogers* (Boston: Little, Brown & Company, 1953); Betty Rogers, *Will Rogers, His Wife's Story* (Indianapolis: Bobbs Merrill, 1941); Donald Day (ed.), *The Autobiography of Will Rogers* (Boston: Houghton Mifflin Company, 1949).

Prince Alexis Lucca, who led the Cossacks in Buffalo Bill's Wild West as early as 1896 (above), was with the 101 Ranch show in England when World War I started in 1914. He left to join the Russian Army and his fate is unknown. Vincenzo (Vincent) Orapeza (below in the center) was expert roper with the Buffalo Bill show and teacher of Will Rogers. Orapeza has been called the top roper of all time.

Courtesy of the Denver Public Library Western Collection.

82

at Brighton Beach, New York, they could advertise "Two Amusement Sensations Combined."[18]

An announcement of this decision in a 1908 courier is headed by pictures of the three Miller brothers and of Edward Arlington. There is no further mention of him, but he probably was responsible for the decision. A veteran of Barnum & Bailey, he had been with Pawnee Bill until Major Lillie decided to spend the 1908 season at Wonderland Park, Boston. Arlington's talents were those of advance man, general agent, and railroad contractor. He possibly was in charge of all show business affairs. His father, George Arlington, was with the show in 1908, and in later years became general manager. After 1910 the show was Miller Bros. & Arlington but show papers have little to say about the Arlingtons.

Although the Millers insisted it was "No circus, but a real Wild West Show," Prince Lucca and his Wild Riding Cossacks appeared in 1908 and for many years thereafter. Wenona, champion rifle shot, and Bertha Thompson, bronco buster, were headlined. The spectacle was "the Historic Massacre of Pat Hennessey and his Party on the Old Chisholm Wagon Trail," July 4, 1874, with a cast including Bull Bear, accredited with being a participant, and W. E. Malaley, prominent in the fight and pursuit of the Cheyennes.

Guy Weadick, "Cheyenne Bill," was with the 101 in 1908, but left the show at Lethridge, Alberta. In 1912 he staged the first Calgary Stampede. After a swing through Canada and the Northwest, the show made an ill-advised tour of Mexico. Joe Miller challenged Mexican bull fighters to duplicate Bill Pickett's bulldogging. When they refused he accepted a bet that Bill would throw a fighting bull, or stay with him for fifteen minutes. Bill fought the bull the full time and clung to the bull's horns for seven and one-half minutes, but the fighting bull's short, thick neck thwarted his bulldoging technique. Poorly handled publicity had led the crowd to believe that the contest challenged the courage of Mexican bullfighters. Bill was pelted with stones and other missiles, and was badly injured by a thrown bottle. Mexican police arrested several of the demonstrators.[19]

[18]*101 Ranch* (Buffalo, N. Y.: The Courier Company, 1905).
[19]*The Mexican Herald*, December 24, 1908. This contemporary account in an English-language newspaper published in Mexico City, while paying tribute to Pickett's "almost unparalleled daring," is objective, and refutes much of the mythology that has grown up around this event. I am indebted to Ronnie C. Tyler of Amon Carter Museum for uncovering this newspaper article.

During the 1912 season the 101 Ranch show traveled 17,280 miles through twenty-two states and three Canadian provinces putting on 421 performances. Yet this tour was not without mishaps. While the show was traveling from Beaver Dam to Milwaukee August 3, a fire broke out among the packed tents. The train stopped near a creek and the fire was extinguished by a bucket brigade, led by cowboy Wayne Beasley. Five nights later, en route to Lancaster, Wisconsin, one section of the train hit a spread rail and four cars were demolished, killing five team horses and five arena horses and injuring thirty more horses. This crippled the show but Joe C. Miller telegraphed the Chicago Stock Yards for replacements and the show moved on to Evanston, Illinois, to pick them up, skipping only the date at Lancaster.[20]

Following in the footsteps of Buffalo Bill, the Miller brothers took the 101 Ranch show to England in 1914 for the Anglo-American Exposition at Shepherd's Bush, London. Queen Alexandra headed a royal party that attended June 25. It was a show of stars: Guy Weadick of Calgary fame; Johnny Baker, arena director — the Buffalo Bill show had closed in 1913 — Chester Byers, roper; Stack Lee, marksman; and an array of champion cowgirls, Lucille Mann, Alice Lee, Mable Olive, Florence Le Due, Lottie Aldridge, and Babe Willets.

There were six months of triumph, and then disaster. At the outbreak of World War I an order dated August 7, 1914, was served on Zack T. Miller declaring that "the horses and vehicles of the 101 Ranch show are to be impressed for public service." Zack begged off six trick horses and was paid £17,000 (about $80,000 then). In the shipping jam he had to book passage as he found it for show personnel. Prince Lucca and his Cossacks returned to Russia and were lost in the fog of war.

[20]Jerry Armstrong, "Picked Up in the Rodeo Arena," *Western Horseman,* XXVIII (March, 1963), 44-45.

FIFTH EPISODE—
Exciting Contests of Skill and Daring

World War I marked the end of the golden era of outdoor show business; all attempts to revive it were short-lived. The railroad circus began a slow decline, as smaller shows became motorized. As the motor replaced the horse, the largest, grandest, richest free street parade ever seen succumbed to city traffic problems, eliminating the band wagon that had passed into folklore, the calliope at the end of the procession, and the hand-carved-ornamented wagons with their sunburst wheels.

One of the early experimenters with motor transport was Charles H. Tompkins, a Forepaugh veteran who started Tompkins Wild West and Frontier Exhibition in 1911 and combined it with Cooper & Whitby's European Circus in 1913. It ended its run in 1914.

Another show that came close to being among the big ones had quite a different background from the 101 Ranch of the Miller Brothers. Vernon C. Seavers, owner of a theatre and an amusement park in Peoria, Illinois, put together a Lone Bill Wild West for the Al Fresco Park in 1908, with Joe Pollock playing Lone Bill. As it went well, he toured it in a dozen Illinois cities on two railroad cars. In 1909 he changed its name to Young Buffalo Wild West with Cal Lavelle and later Joe R. Smith as Young Buffalo. In 1910 the show left Peoria on thirty railroad cars and carried parade equipment and a side show.

Annie Oakley joined the Young Buffalo Wild West in 1911 and toured with it three seasons. Captain Bogardus, Curtis Liston, and Captain O. G. Stevens were other sharpshooters with the show. Stevens was also notable as driver of a twenty-ox team. Colorado Cotton was chief of cowboys. Red Shirt and Flat Iron were Buffalo Bill veterans among the Indians.

In 1911 Colonel Cummins' Wild West and Indian Congress returned from its European tour and in 1912 joined Seavers to form the Young Buffalo Wild West and Col. Fred Cummins' Far East Combined. That year the show played Chicago for two weeks at a different lot each

---

night. The show was sold at the end of the 1913 season, and "strong on grift," according to its historian, lasted only two months of that unlucky year 1914.[1]

Of many shows at the beginning of the decade, only a few lasted into the war years.[2] Buffalo Bill's Wild West and Pawnee Bill's Far East started off in the big money, and Cody, who during his entire show career planned to retire "after just one more good season," decided 1910 would be it, and made a farewell speech in Madison Square Garden. The show grossed a million that year and both partners were free with their profits. Lillie spent $75,000 on his Bungalow Home at his Buffalo Ranch near Pawnee, Oklahoma, and $100,000 more on furnishings — not counting a nearby $55,000 schoolhouse he donated — says a sixteen-page buffalo-head cutout courier-type *Souvenir* of the December, 1910, opening. The *Souvenir* itself added a pretty penny or two to the costs. The furnishings included paintings by Charles Schreyvogel, E. W. Deming, H. H. Cross, Charles H. Stephens, and E. W. Lenders, artists whose work even then did not come cheap. Meanwhile Cody was sinking more gold into his gold mine at Oracle, Arizona, than he ever took out of it.

Buffalo Bill extended his series of "Farewell Exhibitions" through 1910 and 1911, to 1911 and 1912 as profits slid. A rail wreck near Lowell, Massachusetts, scattered elephants, camels, and buffalo over the landscape, but they were lassoed and paraded into Lowell in time for the performance, May 24, 1911. Business was bad in the New England mill towns. In 1912 profits dropped to $125,000.

The Two Bills show started the 1913 season owing $60,000 for

---

[1]Frank J. Pouska, "Young Buffalo Wild West Show," *Bandwagon*, III (May-June, 1959), 15-16, 18; IV (July-August, 1960), 5-6, 19-20.
[2]S. S. Gillespie and R. H. Burns, *Steamboat — Symbol of Wyoming Spirit* (Laramie: University of Wyoming Press, 1952). The Irwin & Hirsig Wild West, which became Irwin Brothers Cheyenne Frontier Days Wild West in 1913 and 1914 (Colonel C. B. and Frank Irwin, Charles Hirsig) was built around the famous bucker Steamboat, which had been tossing riders off its back at Cheyenne since 1902. Perhaps this was the only show with a horse as star. California Frank's All-Star Wild West of 1911 was another Edward Arlington venture. Indian Pete's Wild West combined in mid-season 1911 with W. H. Coulter's Famous Railroad Shows; in 1912 this combination became Cole Brothers Circus; no relation to any later Cole Brothers Circus. The Circle C Ranch Wild West was managed by Lee R. Clark, about 1911-1912. Also extant in 1912 were King Brothers Wild West and the ten-car Prairie Lillie & Nebraska Bill Wild West. Monroe's Mighty Shows & Buffalo Tom's Wild West ran 1912-1914; for 1913-1914 there were the IXL Wild West and Sig Sautelle's Nine Consolidated Railroad Shows (the nine were two circuses, two museums, two menageries, two hippodromes, and one Historical Wild West). Wyoming Bill's Wild West and Circus, 1913-1915, became Welsh Brothers & Lessig's Circus in 1916.

Fast riding was a regular and exciting part of the 101 Ranch
Wild West Show. Whooping cowboys might sprint from behind the
backdrop scenery (above) or they might struggle with their bucking broncos
before they could mount them (below). No chutes were used and in
most instances the cowboys had to have help.
*Emil W. Lenders, photographer; courtesy of the Western
History Collections, University of Oklahoma Library.*

posters, programs, and other show paper — and Cody had borrowed $20,000 from Harry H. Tammen to help pay the bill for winter quarters. Tammen and his partner Frederick G. Bonfils, owners of the *Denver Post*, were notoriously shrewd and sharp operators. Tammen became interested in outdoor show business. He bought a dog and pony show and attached to it the name of the *Post's* sports editor, Otto C. Floto. Seeking a more traditional circus name, he happened upon and employed a William Sells, and the show became the Sells-Floto Circus. Ringling Brothers, owners of the Sells Brothers name, brought suit, but could not stop William Sells from using his name in a circus. Having taken on the "circus trust," Tammen cast his eye on Buffalo Bill's Wild West and Pawnee Bill's Far East. Cody and Lillie were no match for Tammen and Bonfils. When the show played Denver after a hundred successive losing stands in bad weather, the trap was sprung. After much legal maneuvering the show was sold at auction September 15, 1913.

Cody toured the seasons of 1914 and 1915 with the Sells-Floto Circus and Buffalo Bill's Wild West. Karl H. King was bandmaster and he composed and dedicated several numbers: for Cody an intermezzo, *Passing of the Red Man;* a war dance, *On the Warpath,* for the Indian number; and *Wyoming Days* for the cowboy act. Courtney Ryley Cooper, press agent for the show, was another loyal friend. Cody was not happy on the Tammen show, yet at the closing dinner at Fort Worth, Texas, October 14, 1915, he could boast that he had never missed a performance through 366 of them in 183 days over a route of 16,878 miles. He had cleared off his debt to Tammen and hoped for something else.

The Miller brothers had lost the physical assets of their show to England's war effort in 1914, but the personnel was still available and the 101 Ranch could still round up materials for a show when needed. Jess Willard, "a cowboy from Kansas, crack rifle and revolver shot, expert swimmer, never drinks or smokes," became world heavyweight champion April 5, 1915, by knocking out Jack Johnson at Havana, Cuba. He was signed up with his trainer Walter Monaghan for the after-show of the 1915 season of the Miller Bros. & Arlington 101 Ranch Real Wild West. (It was still "Real" Wild West. Only exceptions were a new group of Imperial Russian Cossacks led by Prince Tepho, Australian boomerang throwing by Verne Tantlinger — elsewhere introduced as chief of the cowboys — and three clowns, Bill Caress, Lorette, and Joe Lewis.) Joseph C. Miller had the lead part.

Plate VIII. Pawnee Bill's Historic Wild West

in 1898 featured "beautiful daring Western Girls and Mexican Senoritas" led by
Senorita Rosalia, lower right, in a "contest of equine skill." Cowgirls won equal rights
in Wild West show contests of horsemanship long before their more
civilized sisters won the right to vote.
Color lithograph. 80 x 110 inches.
Courtesy of the Library of Congress.

Iron Tail of buffalo-nickel fame was perhaps the only Indian ever featured on special paper, a huge color poster. Other acts included Hank Durnell, champion roper of South America, cowboys from Headquarters, cowboys from the Bar L Division, cowgirls from the 101 Ranch, Pony Express, stage coach, emigrant train, and pushball on horseback.

After a final argument over the use of his name, Buffalo Bill cut loose from Tammen and made a deal with the Millers, details of which are unclear and unimportant. Oddly enough Jess Willard went out with the Sells-Floto Circus. Cody's last stands were made on a show styled Buffalo Bill (Himself) and 101 Ranch Wild West, Combined, with the Military Pageant Preparedness — presented by the Miller and Arlington Wild West Show Co.

The omission of "Brothers" in the firm name may be significant. There was disagreement among the Millers at this time. Whereas it was Zack who took the show to England in 1914, the name of Joseph C. Miller is the only one listed with the shows of 1915 and 1916.

But the show changed little. The band had a new leader. Professor D. La Blanca was succeeded by Merle Evans, soon to become a fixture on the Ringling Bros.-Barnum & Bailey Circus. Troupes of Japanese and Arabian acrobats and gymnasts were a very small concession to the Far East idea. Preparedness was very much in the air this last summer before the United States entered World War I, despite the slogan "He kept us out of war" that was used for Woodrow Wilson against Charles Evans Hughes in the 1916 Presidential campaign. In the program, however, the stirring "Military Pageant Preparedness" appears to be nothing more exciting than the long familiar "U. S. Artillery Drill" and "Regular Members of the U. S. Calvary in Military Exercises, Athletic Sports, and Horsemanship." There was also a spectacle, "Reproduction of the Battle of Columbus, New Mexico, showing Villa's Attack," which had occurred March 8 of that year — few shows can claim to be that up-to-date. Veterans of the Thirteenth Cavalry, direct from Columbus, were advertised.

There was one city where "preparedness" was not a good word that summer. Chicago's Republican Mayor William Hale Thompson, "Big Bill," had denounced the hue and cry for preparedness after discovering that Chicago was "the sixth German city in the world." There were doves in those days, and press agents took notice of them. Accordingly from August 19 to 27, 1916, Buffalo Bill (Himself) and 101

Ranch Wild West Combined became the Chicago Shan-Kive and Round-Up — with Mayor William Hale Thompson as honorary director general.

Here a Wild West show became an instant rodeo, providing the missing link between these two forms of entertainment. Oddly the word "rodeo" appeared only once in the program, and then with the explanation that it is "another word for round-up." Shan-Kive is inadequately interpreted as Indian for "a good time," and so far as is known made no other appearance in show world lexicography. Considering later development, it is interesting that the program insists that "The Chicago Round-Up is not a Wild West Show, although amusement features are not neglected," ignoring the facts that it had been a Wild West show the previous week and would be again after the Chicago engagement.

The program of events followed rodeo style with conditions (rules) given for trick and fancy roping, steer roping, trick riding, bucking steer riding, bucking mule riding, steer bulldogging, and wild horse race, most of the contests for world championship titles. Johnny Baker was director of contests and events. Contestants were numbered and familiar names appear — Lucille Mulhall, Bill Pickett, Mexican Joe, Hank Durnell, Prairie Lillie, Tom Kirnan, Montana Jack Ray. Colonel Cody was judge supreme; honorary judges included R. H. Russell of Montana, Mayor James Dahlman of Omaha, Burke Burnett of Fort Worth, J. W. Lynch of Ponca City, and J. C. Miller of the 101 Ranch. Another interesting name is the chairman of the entertainment committee, William A. Pinkerton of the Chicago detective agency.

One of the few reports of contest results in Chicago newspapers noted that Bill Pickett and Ed Lindsey were tied at eleven seconds in the first day's bulldogging. Chicago rules stated, "Positively no biting allowed."[3]

The show ended its tour November 4, 1916. William Frederick Cody, Buffalo Bill, died in Denver January 10, 1917. The Miller brothers, including Joseph C., stayed out of show business until 1924. It has been said that they sold the show to Jess Willard. What the 1917 program says is this: Buffalo Bill Wild West Show Co., Inc., Ray

---

[3]*Chicago Shan-Kive and Round-Up Official Souvenir Program,* **August 19 to 27,** 1916, with insert list of participants, has been compared with *Buffalo Bill (Himself) and 101 Ranch Wild West Combined, Magazine and Daily Review,* with insert for Boston engagement, June 12 to 17.

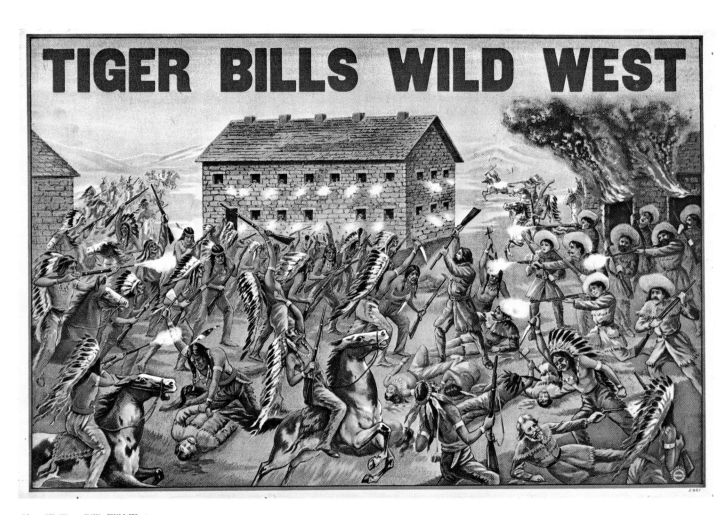

Plate IX. Tiger Bill's Wild West

flourished from 1909 to 1913 under ownership of Dave W. Perrine, and after
that under Emmett D. Snyder, off and on until about 1934. The scene suggests the
"attack on settlers' cabins" that was often the climactic spectacle of the Buffalo
Bill show, but the formidable fort here represented is unidentified.
Color lithograph. 27¾ x 41¾ inches.
Courtesy of J. Edward Leithead Western Americana Collection,
Philadelphia, Pennsylvania.

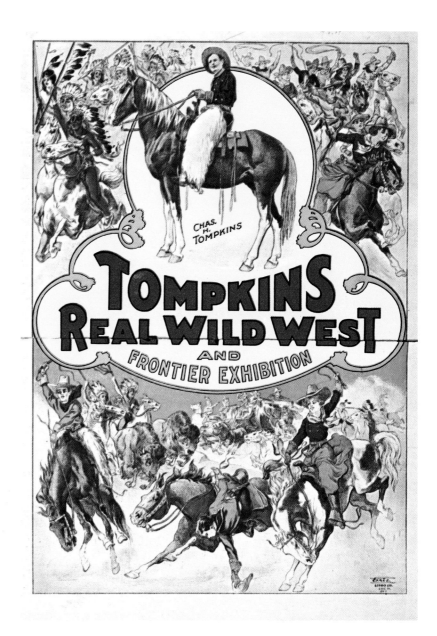

Plate X. Tompkins Real Wild West and Frontier Exhibition

Charles H. Tompkins was a veteran showman, starting as roper in the late 1880's and arena director for the Luella Forepaugh-Fish Wild West in 1903. He formed his own "Real Wild West and Frontier Exhibition" in 1911 and combined it with the Cooper-Whitby Circus owned by Al F. Wheeler for 1913 and 1914. Color lithograph. 28 x 21 inches.
Courtesy of the Denver Public Library Western Collection.

O. Archer presents Jess Willard (Himself in the Flesh) and the Buffalo Bill Wild West Show and Circus. It was much the 101 Ranch show of 1916: Merle Evans was bandmaster; Johnny Baker was arena director and again tried his hand as marksman; Chester Byers and Hank Durnell were champion ropers; the Indians included Iron Cloud and Flying Hawk — Iron Tail died May 28, 1916. The Japanese and Arabian troupes were back; Lorette, the clown; Devlin's Zouaves, the U. S. Artillery Drill, the Pony Express, and the stagecoach holdup. Added were Baby May and Baby Emma, each described in separate events as "the most wonderfully trained elephant in the world," Madam Marantette's high jumping horses, and Rhoda Royal's high school horses.

The show was not the biggest or the best and it is little remembered in annals of show business, but when it folded in 1917, a war year, it was the end of the line. No big Wild West show was extant in 1918; perhaps not even a little one.

The menagerie was another casualty as shows began to transport only performing animals. Mechanization replaced the hordes of roustabouts hired in days of cheap labor. The colorful stake-driving by gangs with sledge hammers was replaced by a machine. Rising costs and increasing popularity of moving pictures cut back all forms of live entertainment.

The parade and the menagerie were hugely expensive elements in the tremendous, self-contained advertising and publicity programs of outdoor shows in the golden age. Newspaper advertising was used and many editors were friendly, but traveling companies were prepared to meet much provincial opposition in the Victorian era. To many church groups all shows and show people were wicked and unproductive time-wasters. Businessmen worried about the money taken out of town by traveling troupes, although dimly realizing that the show people bought some supplies locally, and also drew crowds — there were even special excursions on trains to see the show — and some spectators might spend some of their money on Main Street. Law enforcement officials suspected all shows of grift — the show world's term for short-changing, the shell game, and other gambling cheats to part the unwary from his wallet's contents. Grifters followed all shows, even those that discouraged them, but some small shows depended on grift to break even.

It is no accident that the periodical devoted to the interests of the

Here the wrecking train locomotive, or switch engine, is ready to pull
1101 from the wrecked coach.
Courtesy of Bert Weller, Elmhurst, Illinois.

Train wrecks were among the major perils of outdoor shows. One of the least publicized of those suffered by Buffalo Bill's Wild West occurred April 7, 1904, on the Chicago & North Western Railway a mile west of Melrose Park, Illinois. The Indians entrained at Rushville, Nebraska, and were headed for the docks at Jersey City. Said Luther Standing Bear, interpreter for the group, "We were rounding a curve, when suddenly I saw a train behind us, coming at lightning speed. Then came a terrific crash. There was no time even to cry out. When I opened my eyes again, the seats were piled on top of us and the steam and smoke from the engine were pouring in on us in great clouds. My legs were pinned down, and I was perfectly helpless . . . . I started to sing a brave song." [From Luther Standing Bear, *My People the Sioux*, ed. by E. A. Brininstool (Boston: Houghton Mifflin Company, 1928), pp. 270-271.]

View from north, showing locomotive inside coach. A wrecking train is on
the next track, its caboose at left.
Courtesy of Bert Weller.

outdoor show world was named *The Billboard*. In the golden age bill-boards were boards on which bills were posted. Billposting is almost a lost art in these days of semi-permanent outdoor advertising. There were many billboards in Victorian and Edwardian days. Vacant lots near theatres were lined with them, for melodramas also went in for huge color lithographs of scenes from the play. A youngster touring all his home town's billboards could reconstruct the plot of *The Great Divide, Younger Brothers, The Denver Express,* or *The Texas Cattle King* long before the curtain rose on the production.

Railroad shows had one advance car, sometimes two. The advance man had many duties: leasing the showlot, arranging city licenses when required, contracting for hay to feed horses and groceries for the cook-tent, placing newspaper advertising and trying for free publicity — but one of his main objectives was to plaster the town and immediate vicinity with show bills.

The big weapon in his battery was the twenty-four-sheet, twenty-four times the size of the one-sheet, which was twenty-eight by forty-two inches. The twenty-four-sheet did not come in twenty-four separate pieces, but in six four-sheet sections. That was quite enough for the billposter to work out his jig-saw puzzle of matching the six sections to make one picture. With paste-bucket and a brush with a ten- or twelve-foot handle he first slapped paste on the billboard, then raised a top-corner section on his brush, spotted it in place, and smoothed it out with the brush. Of course he got some paste on the outside of the picture as well as behind it, but that did not seem to matter. He continued until he got the six sheets up, and usually they matched perfectly.

With the one-sheet as base, there were one-half, one, two, three, four, six, eight, twelve, and sixteen sheet posters, in addition to the twenty-four. Up to four-sheet they were printed on one piece of paper; a six was two three-sheets, and the rest were four-sheets.

With this variety almost any surface could be covered — a wooden fence, a barn, an outhouse. Many a farmer welcomed the billposter because the paper covered cracks in the barn or outhouse and might last to keep out next winter's winds. Also he might be bribed with tickets of general admission. The small sheets, up to four-sheet, were used largely in store windows; a vacant store would have all of its glass covered.

Special paper named and pictured show stars such as Annie Oakley

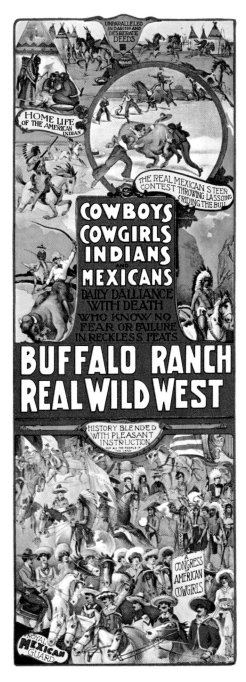

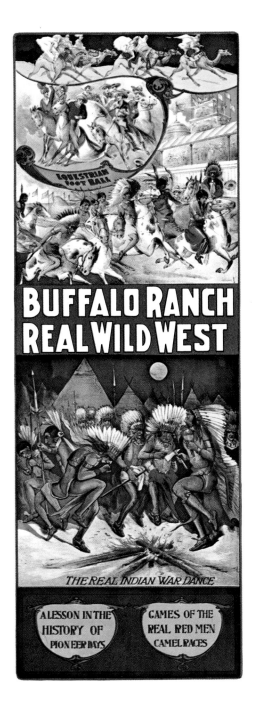

Plate XI. Buffalo Ranch Real Wild West

was a title bandied about under several proprietorships. J. Augusta Jones billed Jones Bros. Buffalo Ranch in 1910. Kit Carson's Buffalo Ranch Wild West, 1911-1914, was unrelated to the historic character, but was owned by Thomas F. Wiedemann. The equestrian foot ball and steer riding shown on these posters suggest the period 1915-1916. A late use was in Harrington's Nickel Plate Circus and Pawnee Bill's Buffalo Ranch Show of 1934. Color Lithographs. Buffalo Ranch Real Wild West — 56 x 21 inches. Buffalo Ranch Real Wild West — Real Indian War Dance — 56 x 21 inches.

Amon Carter Museum Collection.

with the name of the show. Smaller shows bought stock paper with Wild West pictures that could be used for any show; the show's name could be added on order. Then there were date sheets with the name of the town and date of showing.

That was not all. While the billposters were plastering the town the advance agent also saturated the place with handbills. The most common was a single sheet, often printed on both sides in black ink on paper of so cheap a grade that it was dyed bright yellow, green, pink, or blue and commonly called circus paper. These heralds — heralding the coming of the show — might be tacked in bunches at public places where passersby could help themselves, or passed from house to house by small boys, who might earn a ticket to the show with several hours of work.

A more elaborate form of advance advertising was the courier, a booklet often printed in color. The Buffalo Bill show rated well near the top in this department. A thirty-two-page courier copyrighted in 1898 is cut out in the shape of a buffalo head, printed in brown with Cody's picture inset on the front; Cody and Salsbury on the back; the interior printed in green ink. One of 1907 by The Courier Co. of Buffalo — which may have given its name to this form of advertising — was a cut-out of a feathered Indian head in full color with Buffalo Bill superimposed, also thirty-two pages, the interior printing in green. Topping them all was the Buffalo Bill-Pawnee Bill courier of 1909, also a cut-out, of irregular design, with half its pages in full color, reproducing billboard posters and other art work, including Frederic Remington's Buffalo Bill on horseback and Joe Scheurle's portraits of Iron Tail and other Indians. R. Farrington Elwell, famed Arizona painter and magazine illustrator, was among artists employed by Cody as was Robert Lindneux, later a Denver artist widely known for his nature paintings. The famous poster of King Edward VII and the Indian boy was painted by Arthur Jule Goodman.

The Buffalo Bill shows also used a sixteen-page magazine-type courier, about *Saturday Evening Post* size, called the *Rough Rider*. Printed in black on white, it was elaborately illustrated, and contained much information about the show and its features. The *Rough Rider* was started in 1899 and was continued in annual editions into the Buffalo Bill-Pawnee Bill period.[4]

---

[4]*Rough Rider*, IV (8th ed.; Buffalo: The Courier Company, 1907); see also V, 11th ed. for the Buffalo Bill-Pawnee Bill Show. One of 1901 is recorded by Fred D. Pfening, Jr., "Circus Couriers of the Late 1800's," *Bandwagon*, III (January-February, 1959), 3-4.

A Pawnee Bill "Souvenir" of 1893 has full color covers, the "Grand Artillery Race" being featured on the back. His 1907 booklet was called the *Frontier Guide*. Couriers were distributed to newspaper offices, to merchants and supporters of the show, and on occasion, house-to-house.

Quite as elaborate, or perhaps more so were the programs, sold for a dime at the show. Those for Buffalo Bill started with the show itself in 1883 and soon were generously illustrated with color-lithograph covers. One was printed on silk for a Command Performance in London. The program for the Paris show in 1889 had forty-eight pages, largely made up of line drawings, but with some early halftones. By 1893 the halftone had come into its own and the sixty-four page Chicago programs were well printed on a good grade of paper. Most of the text and pictures were about Buffalo Bill, with much about the Ghost Dance outbreak of 1891. The back page showed in color a fantastic Sioux stronghold in the Bad Lands with steeper canyons than even Albert Bierstadt painted. Nate Salsbury, Annie Oakley, and Johnny Baker got a page apiece, but mostly it was Buffalo Bill.

The content remained much the same through 1902 when the show again went overseas, although an advertising wrap-around of sixteen pages was added by 1897. The Paris program of 1905 went to eighty pages, including much about Cody and many illustrations. After the show returned to the United States there was a sharp cutback in program quality; the 1907 "Historical Sketches and Daily Review" being forty-eight pages, more than a quarter advertising, with a local insert of the schedule of events. There was no marked improvement after the Pawnee Bill merger; in fact the advertising proportion increased to almost one-half.

Miller Brothers 101 Ranch used color-lithograph covers on a thirty-two page "Magazine and Daily Review" with one of their best coming in 1927 — but by that time inflation had started; the price went up to fifteen cents. After that the programs were smaller, printed in rotogravure, and given away free. Couriers were magazine style, the later ones in rotogravure.

There was also a surprising amount of book business done on the show lots. P. T. Barnum may have started it with his autobiography, but Buffalo Bill was not far behind. Cody's *Story of the Wild West and Camp-Fire Chats* (1888), and *True Tales of the Plains* (1908), were probably made to be sold on the show, as were John M. Burke's *"Buffalo Bill" from Prairie to Palace* (1893), the anonymous *Buffalo Bill and His Wild West Companions* (ca. 1893), also issued in paperback; and the biography by his sister Helen Cody Wetmore, *Last of the Great Scouts* (1899), which was sold on street corners for $1 with a ticket for the show thrown in. Also selling for $1 were those that obviously were show products: *Thrilling Lives of Buffalo Bill and Pawnee Bill* (1911), by Frank Winch, and *Stirring Lives of Buffalo Bill and Pawnee Bill* (1912), by Frank C. Cooper.

Pawnee Bill's Historic Wild West Company had got into this act as early as 1902 with J. H. De Wolff's *Pawnee Bill: His Experience and Adventures on the Western Plains,* a bound book of 108 pages. A more modest souvenir of the Young Buffalo Wild West and Col. Fred Cummins' Far East Combined, was a ten-cent pamphlet of twenty-four pages, *A Great White Indian Chief,* a biography of Cummins by Richmond C. Hill. In later days *The Life of Tom Mix* was offered, for fifteen cents, as the Souvenir Program of the Sells-Floto Circus in 1931.

Not to be overlooked was the close association of dime novels with the Wild West show business. Here again Buffalo Bill is far in the lead with 1,700 issues containing something like 557 original stories, the rest being reprints. They were by twenty-two authors, including some doubtful pseudonyms. The first one by Ned Buntline was dramatized; he wrote two or possibly three more that enhanced Cody's stage career, and only one that might have been Wild West show publicity, *Will Cody, the Pony Express Rider; or, Buffalo Bill's First Trail* (1885). Prentiss Ingraham wrote during Cody's years in stage melodramas; but he also was nearby when the Wild West started, is credited with writing publicity for it, and put out an increasing number of dime novels as the show succeeded. Ingraham also wrote *Buck Taylor, King of the Cowboys,* following it with a half dozen more, all of them before Taylor left the Buffalo Bill show to start one of his own.

A definite link with show business comes in *Buffalo Bill Stories,* a five-cent weekly started by Street & Smith in 1901, using original stories by Ingraham until his death in 1904, reprints from previous dime-novel libraries, and original stories by several other authors, among them W. Bert Foster. For the issue of July 30, 1910, Foster was commissioned to start a series featuring Major Lillie with Colonel

Plate XII. Iron Tail, America's Representative Indian Chief

Iron Tail of the Oglala Sioux, was with Buffalo Bill's Wild West as early as 1901.
After it folded in 1913, he joined the 101 Ranch show. He was billed as the Indian
on the buffalo nickel, minted from 1913 to 1938. Iron Tail died in 1916 while
with the Buffalo Bill-101 Ranch show.
Color lithograph. 110½ x 40 inches.
*Courtesy of the Jos. Schlitz Brewing Company Collection of
Circus Posters at the Circus World Museum, Baraboo, Wisconsin.*

Cody — at a time when the show was announcing Buffalo Bill's farewell tour and building up Pawnee Bill as his successor. The first story, *Buffalo Bill's Ultimatum; or Facing Terrors with Pawnee Bill*, was launched with considerable fanfare. The masthead was changed to include a medallion with the heads of Cody and Lillie, similar to that used on show paper. From then on to the end of the publication in 1912 Pawnee Bill was the secondary hero. Foster wrote twenty-six of the seventy-four original stories featuring the Two Bills; others were reprints of old stories with Wild Bill Hickok, Texas Jack, White Beaver Powell, or some other companion of Buffalo Bill renamed Pawnee Bill.

Buffalo Bill Stories was succeeded by the *New Buffalo Bill Weekly*, which ran from September 1, 1912, to August 30, 1919, reprinting all the Two Bills stories and continuing their faces on the masthead long after the show's tents had been folded and sold under the auctioneer's hammer, and even beyond the death of Buffalo Bill. So the close connection with show business was limited.

Pawnee Bill, on his own account, had previously been top hero of a dozen or more dime novels by Ingraham, Paul Braddon (who also wrote Buffalo Bill stories), E. W. Wheeler and others. A few more Wild West showmen were named in dime novels, and perhaps others took their show names from the sensational weeklies.

There are also, surprisingly, dime novels about Wild West shows. Nate Salsbury figures in a Beadle's Dime Library title, *Daredeath Dick, the King of the Cowboys; or, In the Wild West with Buffalo Bill*, by Leon Lewis. However, the Wide Awake Library's contribution, *Little Quick Shot; or, Buffalo Bill's Wild West in Europe*, by Paul Braddon, has a boy hero — not Annie Oakley, who seems to have missed dime novel exploitation. *Three Chums Weekly* Number 52 was *Three Chums with Buffalo Bill's Wild West*. Frank Tousey's *Wild West Weekly* perpetrated *Young Wild West's Wild West Show*. Its subtitle *Caught in the European War*, and its sequel, *Young Wild West and the Kaiser; or, The Big Show in Berlin* suggest the 101 Ranch troubles in London in 1914. Most of the list of fifteen or so are about imaginery shows: *Diamond Dick's Wild West, Fred Fearnot's Wild West Show, Ted Strong's Wild West Show*, and *A Game of Bluff; or, The Dalton Gang in a Wild West Show*.

Despite his dominence in dime novels, or perhaps because of it, Buffalo Bill figures little in hard-cover fiction. Mark Twain's *A*

Horse's Tale (1907) is about Buffalo Bill's horse. Allan Vaughan Elston's *Saddle Up for Sunlight* (1952) includes a reference to the Colonel as a resident of Cody, Wyoming. Edwin L. L. Sabin's *Buffalo Bill and the Overland Trail* (1914) is good juvenile fiction of the old school; others are *Red Eagle, Buffalo Bill's Adopted Son,* by M. Moran (1948) and Elmer Sherwood's *Buffalo Bill — The Boys' Friend* (1917), which was split up into two dime-store books with separate titles. There were also two or three Big Little Books and a couple of comic book titles, and several juvenile biographies that could be classed as fiction. Courtney Ryley Cooper made Pawnee Bill the hero of his novel *Oklahoma* (1926).

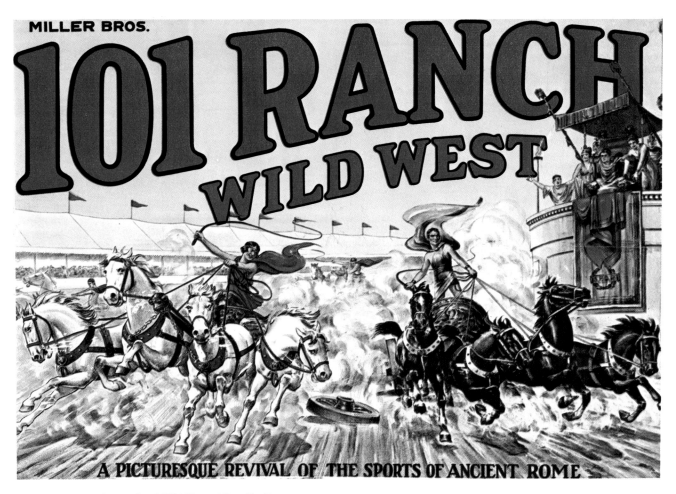

Plate XIII. Miller Brothers 101 Ranch Wild West and Great Far East

"Far East" was a concession to a need for circus acts to augument the limited variety of acts developed for the Wild West. When the show that grew on an Oklahoma ranch went Far East, it went all the way with "the mighty spectacle *Julius Caesar*, dazzling prelude to the show, a spectacle "employing nearly one thousand people and animals," featuring Harriet Hodgini as Cleopatra, dancing on a stage upheld by elephants, Roman light cavalry, gladiators, and the really perilous four-horse chariot race.
Color lithograph. Sight 26 x 21 inches.
Courtesy of George E. Virgines Collection, Elmhurst, Illinois.

SIXTH EPISODE—
A Series of Farewell Exhibitions

Whatever aspect of Wild West shows is considered, the subject matter inevitably comes back to Buffalo Bill. He started the Wild West show and he dominated it; only sporadically did it survive him. The public came as much to see Buffalo Bill as they did to see his show; he was the dime novel hero come to life, and they cared little that he was also authentically the scout and plainsman he was advertised to be. All other shows were imitative, however much they claimed to be the real Wild West or the historic Wild West. And some went so far as to hire an imitation Young Buffalo or Buffalo Ben to take the part.

The only other universally recognized personality who was entirely a product of the Wild West shows was Annie Oakley. Motion pictures, biographies, a couple of comic books, a brief television series, and more especially the Rodgers and Hammerstein *Annie Get Your Gun* helped to keep her name alive. Or did they happen along because her name was alive? Mention Annie Oakley in any gathering and the name will ring a bell—but who remembers Lucille Mulhall, Lillian Smith, May Lillie, Mabel Strickland or Tad Lucas? A part of it is the euphony of the name Annie picked for herself, a part of it was her own superb showmanship, and the rest—who knows?

There were others who served their apprenticeship in the Wild West shows—Will Rogers and Tom Mix for example—but won wider fame elsewhere. Pawnee Bill is not entirely forgotten. As for the others—try these names on your friends: Bill Pickett, Buck Taylor, Johnny Baker, Colonel Fred Cummins, Vincenzo Orapeza (usually misspelled when mentioned), Antonio Esquivel, John Y. Nelson, Guy Weadick, Hank Durnell, and Suicide Ted Elder. All were big names in their day.

In the post-war period the personalities headlined were those who had made their names in the horse operas of Hollywood, and most Wild West programs were part of a circus, or an after-show. Of record in 1920 are the Campbell-Bailey-Hutchinson Circus and Wild

West Combined, which lasted until 1922; Wild Bill's Wild West and Old Cheyenne Frontier Days Combined, which may have toured only in the Hall & Roby Carnival; Barrett Shows and Oklahoma Bill's Wild West; and the Rhoda Royal Circus combined with Old Buffalo Wild West, which in 1922 substituted Oklahoma Ranch Wild West.[1]

Rodeo had an explosion of popularity immediately after World War I, sparked perhaps by Guy Weadick's New York Stampede at Sheepshead Bay in 1916, and the Buffalo Bill-101 Ranch Shan-Kive and Round-Up in Chicago the same year. Calgary's Victory Stampede of 1919 started a new series, divorced in 1923 from the annual Industrial Exhibition to stand on its own feet as the Calgary Exhibition and Stampede. Cheyenne Frontier Days had been going on since 1897. The Pendleton Round-Up started in 1910. Others were the Denver Mountain and Plain Festival, Deadwood Days of '76, and Black Hills Range Days, but rarely, except in California, was the old Spanish word rodeo used. As late as 1922 it was Cheyenne Kiser's Cowboy Round-Up that was a feature of Atlanta's Progress and Prosperity Week.

Tex Austin (John Van Austin) gave a considerable boost to both the word and the idea with the World's Championship Rodeo Contest staged in Chicago's Soldier Field in 1925, and continued as Chicago Rodeo (championship claims cause trouble) through 1926, 1927, and 1928, with Hoot Gibson as added star in 1928. These were big shows, drawing top contenders, and attracted wide attention through the West. Programs to the end were careful to explain that "Rodeo (pronounced Ro-Day'-o) is a Spanish word and means round-up of cattle on the open range." That pronunciation did not hold up too well. Will James, Ross Santee, Owen P. White, Clem Yore, and William H. Hanby wrote articles for Tex Austin's programs. Tex had produced a rodeo at the Empire Exposition at Wembley, England in 1924. He tried again in England in 1934 but with less success. In 1938 he was found dead in the garage of his home in Santa Fe; he had lost his ranch and had come upon hard times.

Madison Square Garden was holding rodeo championship contests in these years, and in addition to the traditional July 4 and County Fair competitions, rodeos were springing up everywhere. Rodeo was called a contest, not an exhibition — Fort Worth claims to be the

[1]Chindahl, *History of the Circus*, p. 242, named Rhoda Royal as proprietor of the Barrett Shows, which seems improbable.

Buffalo Bill standing by the "Deadwood Stage." *Courtesy of the State Historical Society of Colorado.*

original indoor rodeo because it was announced in 1918, "This is to be strictly a contest, not just an exhibition." Contestants paid entry fees and profited only if they won prize money. They paid their own transportation and hospital bills; there was no health insurance for a bronc buster. Rules were not standardized, and neither were the awards of prize money.

In 1929 the Rodeo Association of America was formed to try to make some sense out of the chaos, but real progress came in 1936 when cowboys went on strike in Boston and formed the Cowboy Turtles Association, which became the Rodeo Cowboy Association in 1945. That year a championship award system was created, and five standard events were recognized: saddle-bronc riding, bareback riding, Brahman bull riding, steer wrestling, and calf roping. Approved events include: wild-horse race, wild-cow milking, ribbon roping, steer decorating, double mugging, steer roping, team roping, and team tying. Calgary claims as its own the chuck-wagon race. Some 500 rodeos a year abide by R.C.A. rules.

Most of these events are to be found in the programs of Buffalo Bill's Wild West, the Miller Brothers 101 Ranch, and other Wild West shows. The main difference is that they were done by hired performers instead of by prize-money contestants. But there were also traveling rodeos, presumably with salaried performers. In some cases "rodeo" seems to be substituted for "Wild West" as a more popular drawing card. The Jones-Williamson All Star Rodeo, Hippodrome and Western Attractions, touring in 1935, seemed very much a Wild West show. So was the very colorful and spectacular Flying X Rodeo produced by Colonel A. L. Gatewood in Chicago in 1940. Gene Autry's Flying A Ranch Stampede of 1942 revived much Wild West-Far East tradition with horseback quadrille, Hollywood sky ballet, Roman chariot race, Roman standing race, and exhibition of longhorn steers.

The Real Wild West of Miller Brothers 101 Ranch came back, bigger and better than ever, opening April 21, 1925, at Oklahoma City. The Arlingtons were gone and Tom S. Tucker put the show together. There were forty wagons — a parade was put on in Washington, D.C. as late as 1931.[2] The big top was twice as big as it had been in pre-war years. There was an Arabian spectacle, elephants and camels, elk and buffalo, and such reliables on hand as Hank Durnell,

[2]Pictured in Francis Beverly Kelley, "The Land of Sawdust and Spangles," *National Geographic Magazine*, LX (October, 1931), 464.

Milt Hinkle, and Tad Lucas. Ezra Meeker was there with his ox-team, retracing the Oregon Trail trip he had made originally in 1852. By 1926 "Great Far East" was added to some show paper. The "Sun Goddess" spectacle of 1927 was succeeded in 1928 by a "Julius Caesar" spectacle featuring a four-horse chariot race that remained in the show three years. "Suicide Ted" Elder was advertised in his "suicide leap" Roman riding two horses, standing with a foot on each, and jumping over a motor car full of passengers. The attack on the wagon train was variously billed as the "Mountain Meadows Massacre" and the "Death Valley Massacre." Theodore Govorchin, wrestler taking on all comers, was the concert attraction in 1927. Jack Hoxie of the movies and his leading lady Dixie Starr were on hand in 1930.

It was a big show, and apparently a deserving one, but in financial trouble almost from the start. Whereas the Miller brothers had ended their 1908-1916 tours $800,000 ahead, the new show dropped $119,000 in 1926 and the Depression was yet to come. Joe Miller died October 21, 1927, overcome by carbon monoxide gas while working on his car in his garage. George L. Miller died in an auto accident on an icy road February 1, 1929. Bill Pickett died more appropriately when a horse fell on him in 1932. Creditors stopped the show in Washington, D.C. August 5, 1931. Loss of the ranch followed.

Zack T. Miller, the surviving brother, never quite gave up. Chicago's World Fair of 1933 — A Century of Progress — seemed to offer opportunity to try for Buffalo Bill's triumph at the 1893 fair. Zack Miller put together a good show, but it was at the south end of the fairgrounds, and few customers got that far. (The writer counted a house of only eight one afternoon.) Its run was short. The Original Miller Brothers 101 Ranch with Zack Miller in person tried again in Los Angeles in 1945 with backing by N. Edward Beck and Ralph Ravenscroft, but the show dropped $35,000 in two days. Milt Hinkle was producer. Milt learned bulldogging from Bill Pickett and was tops at that art until he tried it from an airplane at Nuevo Laredo, Mexico, in 1931. He came out of it badly crippled and turned to producing and promoting. In 1946 Jimmie Wood reorganized the 101 Ranch Wild West Circus at Venice, California, one-time winter quarters of the Miller Brothers, opening at Santa Monica. In 1949 Zack Miller was touring the South with a 101 Ranch Show when he was jailed for refusing to pay a fine for speeding. He kept staging exhibitions until his death January 3, 1952.

There were others. Wheeler Brothers Greater Shows and Famous Stampede Wild West, owned by Elmer H. Jones and managed by Al F. Wheeler was on tour in 1921. In 1932 Leo Snyder was manager of Wheeler Shows and Tiger Bill's Wild West. Allen Brothers Wild West, Charles and Mert H. Allen, was extant 1929-1934. Buck Jones Wild West started in California in 1929 but did not last the season. Harrington's Nickel Plate Circus and Pawnee Bill's Buffalo Ranch toured in 1934, perhaps the last for the Pawnee Bill name, although Colonel Hank Linton was advertised as "former pal of the great Pawnee Bill" while putting on a concert for the Cole Brothers Circus of 1944. Colonel Preston, "late of Texas Rangers," put on ten minutes of Wild West for the Hagenbeck-Wallace & Forepaugh-Sells Brothers Combined Circus of 1937 — one of the truly imposing names in show business, pulled out of the trunkful of names owned by Ringlings.

Ken Maynard put some of his Hollywood earnings into Maynard's Diamond K Ranch Wild West and Circus in 1936, and in 1938 was billed as Cole Brothers Circus with Clyde Beatty and Ken Maynard. One of the most successful of Hollywood stars in show business was Tom Mix. Tom Mix was employed in the dude ranch department of the 101 Ranch in the early days of the century and learned to tell tall tales. Perhaps in this category were his reports of service in the Spanish-American War, the Philippines, Boxer War in China, and the Boer War. Will Rogers is said to have taken him to task for his "yarning." They were together in the celebrated roping of a steer in the audience at Madison Square Garden in 1905, although Will had listed his pal as "Tom Mixico" on the program, and so it appeared in resultant publicity. In 1907 Elinor Glynn, of *Three Weeks* fame, called Tom her "ideal man," but the publicity man slipped again and it came up "Nix." There was no doubt about Tom Mix's ability when he hit Hollywood in 1910; he and his horse Tony became the idols of a generation of Saturday afternoon movie-goers. Mix was with the Sells-Floto Circus in 1931. He organized his own Tom Mix Circus and Wild West in 1935, which ran through three seasons. He was killed October 11, 1940, in an auto accident near Florence, Arizona.

Radio contributed one Wild West hero to show business, the long-lived Lone Ranger. Brace Beemer, who wore the black mask longest in the quarter-century serial originated by WXYZ, Detroit, appeared

Behind the scenes at the 101 Ranch Wild West Show. *Vince Dillon, photographer; courtesy of the Western History Collections, University of Oklahoma Library.*

in the 11th Annual Olympia Circus at Chicago Stadium and made other publicity appearances. Perhaps the most widely known of the after-show performers was Colonel Tim McCoy, who had the concert with the Ringling Brothers and Barnum & Bailey Combined Shows in 1935, 1936, and 1937.

Timothy J. McCoy was an authentic cowboy and an authentic colonel. Few showmen could legitimately make those claims, although many did. Born in Saginaw, Michigan, April 10, 1891, and educated in Chicago, he took off for Lander, Wyoming, as a youngster, worked as cowpoke, and filed a homestead claim on a ranch in the Owl Creek country. He took officer candidate training at the beginning of World War I, was commissioned captain of cavalry, and later was promoted to lieutenant colonel. Major General Hugh L. Scott, former chief of staff, was impressed with McCoy's knowledge of the sign language that he had learned from the Arapahos and Shoshones. After the war McCoy served as adjutant general of Wyoming with the rank of brigadier general.[3]

McCoy resigned in 1922 to become technical director in charge of Indians for Jesse L. Lasky's *The Covered Wagon*. He took the Indians on tour to exploit the famous silent film, and did so well at it that Metro-Goldwyn-Mayer signed him to do a series of Westerns starting with *War Paint* in 1925. He was a top Western star for ten years before taking on the Ringling concert Wild West. During those years he dreamed of his own Wild West show after the manner of the great years of Buffalo Bill and the 101 Ranch. He had miniature models constructed, later carried out in full scale by Hollywood scene painters.

Colonel Tim McCoy's Real Wild West and Rough Riders of the World took the road in 1938, the last all-new railroad show. All of its wagons were especially built to its specifications. A pneumatic stake driver was invented for the show. Its hospital unit was designed by Dr. A. C. Furstenberg, of the University of Michigan's College of Medicine, and staffed by volunteers from that school on a vacation schedule. (Only one doctor got such a vacation.) The show opened April 14 in the International Amphitheatre in Chicago. The Grand Entry was spectacular. The spectacle, "The Winning of the West," depicted the driving of the golden spike with elaborate scenery and

[3]A photograph of Jack Wilson and General T. J. McCoy appears in Hugh Lenox Scott, *Some Memories of a Soldier* (New York: Century Company, 1928), facing p. 88.

Headin' for the Show Grounds. Unloading the show was no small task when Buffalo Bill's Wild West was making one and two-night stands in its later years. *John C. Hemment, New York, photographer; courtesy of the Denver Public Library Western Collection.*

Soup's on at the Buffalo Bill's Wild West grounds. *John C. Hemment, photographer; courtesy of the Denver Public Library Western Collection.*

prop replicas of the locomotives. Some saw it as the finest scene ever done in an outdoor show; to others the pageantry fell flat.

The show had many of the traditional features, the Pony Express, the Deadwood stagecoach, the covered wagons, cavalry drill, trick riding by Cossacks, gauchos, and Bengal lancers. Celebrities included Al Jennings, former bandit; Tex Cooper, "Arizona Bill," Captain Jim Moore, and Silver Tip Baker. Unlike the Miller Brothers, however, McCoy had little of the contest-type events that were making rodeo a popular spectacle. There was no bulldogging or steer riding. McCoy himself, roping eight horses with one loop, drew acclaim, but there were few thrill acts.

The thirty-car show train moved the Wild West to Columbus, Dayton, Cincinnati, Parkersburg, and Washington. Attendance was light. The side show was an Indian village, apparently a good museum piece, but it flopped and was dropped. The last three railroad moves were made on credit. When business failed to pick up in Washington, creditors took over and threw the show into receivership on May 5. The last great Wild West show played less than a month.

Among reasons given for the failure was a lack of paper — the color-lithograph coverage that was the mainstay of show publicity in the golden era of the outdoor show. Joseph Scheuerle had been employed to design the show paper, but slow pay delayed its delivery and Clint W. Finney, general agent, rounded up stock paper with Wild West pictures to fill out. But even with this help Chicago billboards showed little of Tim McCoy's Wild West, and it was much the same the rest of the route. There was opposition billing from Cole Brothers, Hagenbeck-Wallace, and Ringling for dates not far behind the Wild West, but perhaps this could have been overcome had the advance car had better backing. Press agents complained that even the press books were late. Most of the money was spent on equipment, leaving little to run the show.[4]

However, 1938 was a bad year for outdoor shows, and Tim McCoy was not the only victim. The Tom Mix Circus and Wild West folded that year, as did Robbins Brothers Circus, which had Hoot Gibson's Wild West as concert. Hagenbeck-Wallace was stopped, never to go on the road again. Ringling went to the barn in June because of a

[4]Fred D. Pfening, Jr., *Col. Tim McCoy's Real Wild West and Rough Riders of the World* (Columbus: Pfening & Snyder, 1955); *Col. Tim McCoy's Real Wild West Magazine and Daily Review* (1938); *Ringling Bros. and Barnum & Bailey Circus Magazine and Daily Review* (1935), p. 44.

Roman Riding — standing on two bareback horses at racing speed — is difficult; on three horses is uncommon; on four horses is rare indeed. The rider is believed to be Clarence Schultz, veteran of the 101 Ranch. The photograph was taken during the 1916 Chicago engagement of the Buffalo Bill - 101 Ranch Show, near the entry, with somewhat phony-looking scenic mountain in background.

Courtesy of Fred B. Hackett, Chicago.

strike, and Al G. Barnes & Sells-Floto, which replaced it, had the final use of those circus names. Other casualties were Seils-Sterling Big Four Ring Circus, Wild West, and Animal Review, and Harris Brothers.

Like Zack Miller, Tim McCoy declined to quit; he has continued trouping, for several years heading a Wild West show that was part of the Carson and Barnes Circus. There have been others — the Austin Brothers Three Ring Circus and Real Wild West of 1945, for example — but none that could boast, "No circus, but a real Wild West show."

SEVENTH EPISODE—
The Final Salute: An Historically Authentic Depiction

Is the Wild West show an obsolete form of entertainment? The popularity of rodeo, its legitimate successor, refutes it. Few of the features that made Buffalo Bill's Wild West unique American entertainment have disappeared. "Custer's Last Fight" was postponed because of rain at Crow Agency, Montana, in 1969, but the spectacle that the Buffalo Bill show played so often, continued to draw crowds a week later. The Schlitz Circus Parade in Milwaukee July 4, 1969, had a Wild West section portraying Buffalo Bill and Annie Oakley, a stagecoach, a covered wagon, and the Pawnee Bill bandwagon. A close look at the programs for Cheyenne, Calgary, Pendleton, and half a thousand more rodeos will show many events that parallel the Buffalo Bill show or the 101 Ranch besides "Cowboy Fun" that developed into the prize contests.

But the survival is not nearly as important as the original impact. It was the Wild West show that dramatized the American West as a place of romance and glamour. Particularly was this so in Europe where the Buffalo Bill influence can still be traced more directly and dime novels about Buffalo Bill are still being written and sold, even in Germany despite two wars in which the United States was the enemy. The dime novel added to the glorification, but it was closely related to the Wild West show. Owen Wister's *The Virginian* was ancestor to Zane Grey and the type "Western" that created a land of legendry that never existed.

Before Buffalo Bill the cowboy was no hero. President Chester A. Arthur in his 1881 message to Congress denounced a band of "armed desperadoes known as 'Cowboys'" as menaces to the peace of Arizona, and the same President Arthur was threatened with kidnaping by "a party of Cowboys" during a trip West in 1883. The working cowboy of that period, the "hired man on horseback," saw little of Billy the Kid and less of the glamour that was soon to attach to his boredom. Buffalo Bill printed Texas Jack's defense of the cowboy in his programs and couriers and created the first cowboy hero, Buck Taylor, who was King of the Cowboys in the Wild West show before becoming fictional hero in Prentiss Ingraham's dime novel with the same title. It is noteworthy that the fictional Buck Taylor had as little to do with cows as Owen Wister's *The Virginian*. So quickly was the romantic, ideal cowboy accepted in the West that the artist Burleigh Withers, who lived in the Medicine Bow country before and and after, used to say of criticism of the unrealistic language of Mr. Wister's cowboys, "Well, maybe we didn't talk that way before Mr. Wister wrote his book, but we sure all talked that way after the book was published."

Buffalo Bill not only started the cowboy hero on his way, he also, surprisingly, changed the concept of the Indian. J. Frank Dobie noted that

> Heroizing Andrew Jackson as a fighter against unhorsed Indians east of the Mississippi became obsolete even before boys ceased to read the romances of James Fenimore Cooper. The whole tradition of Indians fighting afoot has faded from the popular mind. On the other hand the tradition of fighting the wild-riding Indians of the West remains on screen and in pulp fiction almost as alive as it was when Buffalo Bill's arena presented it in pageant form.[1]

Buffalo Bill employed Sioux mostly; they rode horses and wore feathered headdresses. Apaches wore no feathers and seldom rode horses, but when Hollywood glamorized Cochise and Geronimo, the movie-makers put feathered headdresses on them and they rode horses. It would not be surprising to see a pageant Pocahontas leap from her cayuse to rescue Captain John Smith, or feathered Indians riding their horses to the beach to meet the Pilgrim Fathers at Plymouth Rock, or William Penn at the Delaware Gap.

The Wild West show in its beginning was a representation of a historical era that was still contemporary. As time went on dramatization continued the illusion, as did the accompanying popular literature and its translation to movie and television. The resultant legendary West derived in large part from the Wild West show. The melodramas, the movies, and the television serials were not drama; the dime novel and the "Western" fiction were not literature; the twenty-four-sheet lithograph was not art. Yet each left an impress on the American scene that cannot be ignored. The song the cowboy sang to the herds on the bedground has become a part of our heritage, and so are the heralds, the couriers, and the posters that announced the coming of the Wild West show to bring a day

[1]J. Frank Dobie, *The Mustangs* (Boston: Little, Brown and Company, 1952), p. 43.

of ever-remembered glamour to break a dull and dreary monotony.

In these days of few illusions and fewer heroes, perhaps we should recall that once we had both — and were happier. Buffalo Bill's cowboy fun was an event that might merit revival.

Checklist of Wild West Shows

This list has been compiled from many sources over many years and probably is incomplete. It includes circus and Wild West combinations, which are not very different from "Wild West and Far East"; some concerts or after-shows, which are not always different from circus and Wild West combinations; and some touring rodeos, which are not much different from the Cheyenne Frontier Days Wild West of earlier days. The total is 116, which includes some combinations where the shows are also listed separately, some changes of name that may be essentially the same show, and some cases where the same name was used by different shows.

1. Fred Akins Real Wild West and Far East Show
   1909-10, toured Australia
2. Allen Bros. Wild West
   1929-34, Charles and Mert H. Allen
3. Arlington & Beckman's Oklahoma Ranch Wild West
   1913, Edward Arlington and Fred Beckman
4. Austin Bros. 3 Ring Circus and Real Wild West
   1945
5. Gene Autry's Flying A Ranch Stampede
   1942
6. Barrett Shows and Oklahoma Bill's Wild West
   1920
7. Bee Ho Gray's Wild West
8. Broncho John, Famous Western Horseman and His Corps of Expert Horsemen
   1906, J. H. Sullivan
9. Buckskin Ben's Wild West and Dog and Pony Show
   1908-13, Benjamin Stalker
10. Buckskin Bill's Wild West
    1900
11. Buckskin Joe's Realistic Wild West
    1891, Edward Jonathan Hoyt
12. Buffalo and Wild West
    1902
13. Buffalo Bill and Dr. Carver's Wild West
    1883, William F. Cody, W. F. Carver

14. Buffalo Bill's Wild West
    1884-1908, Cody, Nate Salsbury; Adam H. Bogardus, 1884 only; James A. Bailey after 1895
15. Buffalo Bill's Wild West and Pawnee Bill's Far East Combined
    1909-13, Cody, Gordon W. Lillie
16. Buffalo Bill (Himself) and 101 Ranch Wild West Combined
    1916, Miller and Arlington Wild West Show Co.
17. Buffalo Tom's Wild West
18. California Frank's All-Star Wild West
    1911, Edward Arlington, C. F. Hafley, Major Rhodes
19. Campbell-Bailey-Hutchinson Circus and Wild West Combined
    1920-22, A. G., W. P., Anna N. Campbell, Fred Bailey Hutchinson, Alberta and Julia W. Hutchinson
20. Carlisle's Wild West
    1909, R. C. Carlisle
21. Carver and Crawford Wild West
    1883-85, W. F. Carver, Captain Jack Crawford; J. J. McCafferty
22. Dr. W. F. Carver's Wild America
    1889-93
23. Cherokee Ed's Wild West
    1909 only, Ed Baumeister
24. Circle C Ranch Wild West
    1911-12, Lee R. Clark
25. Circle D Ranch Wild West and Cooper Bros. Famous Shows
    1914
26. Cole Bros. Circus with Clyde Beatty and Ken Maynard
    1938
27. Colorado Grant's Wild West
28. J. R. Cortine's Wild West
    1885, W. Hennessy
29. W. H. Coulter Shows and Indian Pete's Wild West
    1911, only W. H. Coulter, William Hooganwoning, George H. Embree
30. Coup and Carver's Wild West
    1884, W. C. Coup, Dr. W. F. Carver
31. Col. Frederic T. Cummins Indian Congress
    1898-1904

32. Cummins Wild West and Indian Congress
    1905-11; combined with Young Buffalo, 1912
33. Barney Damerest's Wild West
34. Diamond Bar Ranch Wild West
    1909
35. Dickey's Circle D Ranch Wild West
    1909
36. W. W. Dillingham's Wild West (Dare Devil Dillie)
37. Fargo & Company
    1885
38. Flying X Rodeo
    1940, Col. A. L. Gatewood
39. Adam Forepaugh's New and Greatest All-Feature Show and
    Wild West Combination
    1887-89, Dr. W. F. Carver featured 1887-88
40. Luella Forepaugh-Fish Wild West
    1903
41. Gabriel Brothers Champion Long-Distance Riders Wild West
    1904
42. Harrington's Nickel Plate Circus and Pawnee Bill's Buffalo
    Ranch
    1934
43. Hart & Schofield Indian Show
    1885
44. Ben Holmes Wild West
    1914
45. Hunter & McKinney Combination
46. Indian Bill's Wild West
    1903, J. A. Jones
47. Indian Bill's Wild West and Cole & Rogers Circus Combined
    1906, J. A. Jones
48. Indian Pete's Wild West
    1911, Boyd & Culbertson; combined with W. H. Coulter
    July 26, 1911
49. Irwin and Hirsig Wild West Show
    1910, Col. C. B. Irwin, Charles Hirsig
50. Irwin Bros. Cheyenne Frontier Days Wild West
    1913-14, Col. C. B. and Frank Irwin
51. IXL Wild West
    1913-14, Jack W. King

52. Buck Jones Wild West
    1929, May-July only
53. Jones Bros. Buffalo Ranch Wild West
    1910, J. Augusta Jones
54. Jones-Williamson All-Star Rodeo, Hippodrome, and Western Attractions
    1935
55. Kemp Sisters Wild West
    1896
56. Kennedy Bros. Wild West
    1893, W. H. Kennedy
57. Kennedy's XIT Ranch
58. King Bros. Wild West
    1912
59. King & Franklin's Wild West
    1887
60. Kit Carson's Buffalo Ranch Wild West
    1911-14, Thomas F. Wiedemann. Succeeded Jones Bros.
61. Cal. Hank Linton, concert, Cole Bros. Circus
    1944
62. Lone Bill's Wild West
    1908, Vernon C. Seavers; Lone Bill was Joe Pollock. Became Young Buffalo, 1909
63. Lone Star May's Wild West
    1909
64. P. Matally's Wild West
    1908-09, Buenos Aires
65. Ken Maynard's Diamond K Ranch Wild West and Circus
    1936
66. McCaddon's International Shows and Wild West
    1905, France, J. T. McCaddon
67. John J. McCafferty Wild West
68. Col. Tim McCoy's Real Wild West and Rough Riders of the World
    1938, April 14-May 4
69. Col. Tim McCoy's Wild West Exhibition, concert, Ringling Bros. and Barnum & Bailey Combined Shows
    1935-37
70. Mexican Joe's Wild West
    1888, London

71. Miller Bros. 101 Ranch Real Wild West
    1907-16, 1925-31, 1933, 1945, 1946, 1949. George L., Joseph
    C., Zack T. Miller, Edward and George Arlington, 1908-16;
    N. Edward Beck and Ralph Ravenscroft, 1945; James Lenox
    Wood, 1946; show's title varied from year to year: Miller
    Bros. & Arlington, 1914-15; "101 Ranch" put ahead, 1908,
    1926, 1928, 1931; "and Great Far East" added 1926-27.
72. Missoula Buffalo's Wild West
73. Tom Mix Circus and Wild West
    1935-38
74. Monroe's Mighty Shows and Buffalo Tom's Wild West
    1912-14, A. M. Cauble
75. Col. Zack Mulhall's Wild West
    1899-1905; 1910-15
76. Noxon's Wild West and Hippodrome
77. O'Dell's Famous Hippodrome and F. J. McCarthy's Arizona
    Wild West
    1893
78. Olympia Circus Starring The Lone Ranger and His Horse
    Silver
    1939, Chicago. (Brace Beemer)
79. Pawnee Bill's Historic Wild West
    1888, 1890-1908. Gordon W. Lillie; "and Great Far East"
    added 1905; combined with Buffalo Bill, 1909-13.
80. Prairie Lillie and Nebraska Bill's Wild West
    1912, Welsh Bros.
81. Idaho Bill Pearson's Wild West
82. Col. Preston, late of Texas Rangers, Ten Minutes of Wild West,
    concert, Hagenbeck-Wallace and Forepaugh-Sells Bros. Combined
    Circus
    1937
83. The Great Rhoda Royal Australian Railroad Shows (Captain
    Walter C. Sharp's Troop of Rough Riders)
    1900-01
84. Rhoda Royal 2 Ring Circus, Hippodrome, and Wild West (in-
    door)
    1913
85. Rhoda Royal Trained Wild Animal (3 Ring Circus; World-toured
    Shows) and Old Buffalo Wild West
    1919-21. Rhoda Royal, Darwin C. Hawn, Harry "Kid" Hunt

86. Rhoda Royal 3 Ring Circus combined with Oklahoma Ranch Wild West
    1922
87. Captain C. W. Riggs' Wild West
88. Robbins Circus with Hoot Gibson's Congress of Rough Riders, Indians and Cossacks
    1938
89. Sig Sautelles Nine Consolidated Railroad Shows — 2 circuses, 2 museums, 2 menageries, 2 hippodromes, and Historical Wild West
    1913-14
90. Sells-Floto-Buffalo Bill (Himself) Shows
    1914-15. H. H. Tammen and F. G. Bonfils
91. Sells-Floto Circus and Tom Mix
    1931
92. Capt. Ed Senechal's Wild West
    1904
93. Skakel & Martin
    1885
94. Snyder Bros. Wild West
    1909
95. Dick Stanley's Wild West
96. Stowe & Long's Circus, Menagerie, Wild West & Balloon Shows
    1889
97. Sutton's American Wild West and Roman Hippodrome
    1890
98. Buck Taylor's Wild West
    1894
99. Texas Bill's Wild West
    1904
100. Texas Bud's Wild West
    1909, P. J. Snell
101. Texas Jack's Wild West
    1903, South Africa
102. Texas Kidd's Reproduction of Frontier Days
    1912-1957. Virgil P. Nuckols; Reno J. Nuckols and Grafton N. Nuckols
103. Tiger Bill's Wild West
    1909-13, Dave W. Perrine; 1914-34, Emmett D. Snyder
104. Tompkins Real Wild West and Frontier Exhibition
    1911-12. Charles H. Tompkins

105. Tompkins Wild West and Cooper-Whitby Circus
    1913-14. Charles H. Tompkins and Al F. Wheeler
106. Col. Uden's Wild West
107. Wheeler Bros. Greater Shows and Famous Stampede Wild West
    1921. Elmer H. Jones, Al F. Wheeler
108. Wheeler Shows and Tiger Bill's Wild West
    1932. Leo Snyder
109. Wild Bill's Wild West and Old Cheyenne Frontier Days Combined
    1920, Hall & Roby (may have toured as Hall & Roby Carnival)
110. Jess Willard (Himself in the Flesh) and the Buffalo Bill Wild West Show and Circus
    1917, "Ray O. Archer presents"
111. Wyoming Bill's Wild West and Circus
    1913-14, Welsh Bros.; became Welsh Bros. & Lessig's Circus, 1915-16
112. Yankee Robinson 3 Ring Circus and Texas Bill's Wild West
    1911-12, Fred Buchanan
113. Young Buffalo Wild West
    1909-11, Vernon C. Seavers (Cal Lavelle was Young Buffalo)
114. Young Buffalo Wild West and Col. Cummins Far East Combined
    1912-14, Vernon C. Seavers, Col. Fred T. Cummins
115. Scout Younger's Wild West
116. Cole Younger and Frank James Wild West
    1903, 1908

Bibliography

Bibliography and Acknowledgments

This being apparently the first attempt at a history of Wild West Shows, it is by necessity based on original sources. The primary material is contemporary advertising, posters, couriers, heralds, and newspaper articles. Such material is extremely elusive, and no one is likely to find enough of it to fill out a complete story — and of course every word and picture is to be viewed with suspicion, as press agents of the outdoor show world are notorious for exaggeration.

Buffalo Bill programs for nearly every year of the show's existence — some dates are doubtful — have been consulted. The Western History Department of the Denver Public Library has the largest collection I have seen. Couriers and heralds are even less common, but a number were located. Miller Brothers 101 Ranch has been covered by programs or couriers for most years. George E. Virgines has a large collection. Pawnee Bill material is fairly common, and a few items showed up from Forepaugh, Young Buffalo, Cummins, Tompkins, and a few others. J. Edward Leithead, in addition to providing information on dime novels, loaned two programs and a real rarity, a Tiger Bill poster.

Newspaper articles are omitted in the bibliography, although a few are cited in notes. Nebraska State Historical Society, Denver Public Library, and Arizona Pioneers Historical Society have collections of clippings and scrapbooks relating to Buffalo Bill. My own collection runs about seventy inches of vertical-file material, mostly clippings, by any count too many to be listed here.

Buffalo Bill bibliography is far too voluminous to be included and is limited to items having Wild West show interest.

The magazine entries include many reminiscent articles that require a "handle with care" warning, but are quite useful where little else is available. Many of the magazines cited are rarely found in library stacks of bound volumes. Much information was derived from stray bits in *Billboard*, *Bandwagon*, and *White Tops* in addition to articles listed.

Much of my obligation goes to those who helped with *The Lives and Legends of Buffalo Bill*. Of more recent date, thanks should go to Mrs. Willa Doty, Research Library, Oklahoma Historical Society; Mrs. Alys Freeze, Western History Department, Denver Public Library; Richard Frost, Buffalo Bill Historical Center, Cody, Wyoming; Fred H. Garlow, grandson of William F. Cody; Fred B. Hackett, Milt Hinkle, Red Fox, Joseph G. Rosa, George LeRoy, Sr., Scout's Rest Ranch State Historical Park, North Platte, Nebraska; Paul D. Riley, Nebraska State Historical Society; Gene Russell; Robert L. Parkinson, Superintendent of Historic Collections, Circus World Museum, Baraboo, Wisconsin; Jack D. Haley, Assistant Curator, and Pat Cathcart, Research Assistant, Western History Collections, University of Oklahoma, Norman; Miss Betty King, Hertzberg Circus Collection, San Antonio Public Library.

Acton, Mildred Mulhall. "Lucille Mulhall — The Original Cowgirl," *The Ranchman*, I (February, 1942), 6-7.

Armstrong, Jerry. "Picked Up in the Rodeo Arena," *Western Horseman*, XXVIII (March, 1963), 44-45.

Baldwin, Dick. Editor. "Powders I Have Known," by Annie Oakley, *Guns & Ammo*, XI (September, 1967), 42-43, 52-54, 56-57.

Barnum, P. T. *Struggles and Triumphs*. New York: Macmillan, 1930.

Beardsley, J. L., "Buffalo Bill Ends an Indian War," *Real West*, XI (January, 1968), 28-29, 58.

Beasley, M. Robert, "The 1,000-Mile Horse Race," *Great West*, II (October, 1968), 30-33.

Beitz, Les. *Treasury of Frontier Relics*. New York: Edwin House, 1966.

Beitz, Lester U. "The Original Deadwood Stage," *Frontier Times*, XL (January, 1966) 41, 58.

Bowen, Elbert H. "The Circus in Early Rural Missouri," *Missouri Historical Review*, XLVII (October, 1952), 1-17.

Bradbury, Joseph T. "Campbell-Bailey-Hutchinson Circus," *Bandwagon* (May-June, 1960), 3-9, 12-17.

_____. "The Rhoda Royal Circus, 1919-1922," *Bandwagon* (May-June, 1961), 3-19.

Buffalo Bill and His Wild West Companions. Chicago: M. A. Donohue & Co., Henneberry Co., n.d.

Burchardt, Bill. "A Rider of the 101," *Oklahoma Today*, XVII (Autumn, 1967).

_____. "The South American Kid," *Oklahoma Today*, XVIII (Autumn, 1968), 4, 28-30.

Burke, John. *Buffalo Bill, from Prairie to Palace*. Chicago: Rand, McNally, 1893.

Bushell, William. *The Life of Captain Adam Bogardus*. Lincoln, Ill., 1956.

Carney, Peter P. *Greatest of Modern Dianas*. Pinehurst, N.C., n.d.

Cattermole, E. G. *Famous Frontiersmen, Pioneers, and Scouts*. Chicago and New York: M. A. Donohue & Co., n.d.

Chambers, Julius. *News Hunting on Three Continents*. New York: Mitchell Kennerley, 1921.

Cheney, Louise. "Annie Oakley, Little Miss Sureshot," *Real West*, X (November, 1967), 20-21, 53-57.

_____. "Lucile Mulhall, Fabulous Cowgirl," *Real West*, XII (March, 1969), 13-15, 58-59, 73.

_____. "Mr. Rodeo Himself: Milt Hinkle," *Real West*, XII (June, 1969), 22-24, 58-59, 64, 74.

Chindahl, George L. *A History of the Circus in America*. Caldwell, Idaho: Caxton Printers, Ltd., 1959.

Clancy, Foghorn. *My Fifty Years in Rodeo*. San Antonio: Naylor Co., 1952.

Clark, Helen. "Steamboat and Midnight — An Incomparable Pair," *Golden West*, V (November, 1968), 36-38, 64-66.

Clemens, Samuel L. [Mark Twain]. "A Horse's Tale," *Harper's Monthly*, CXIII (August-September, 1906), 328-342, 539-549.

Coburn, Walt. "The Inimitable Breezy Cox," *True West*, XV (September, 1967), 14-17, 54-57.

_____. "Tom Mix's Last Sundown," *Frontier Times*, XLII (August-September, 1968), 6-11, 48.

Cody, Louisa Frederici, and Courtney Ryley Cooper. *Memories of Buffalo Bill*. New York and London: D. Appleton & Co., 1919.

Cody, William Frederick. *The Adventures of Buffalo Bill*. New York and London: Harper & Brothers, 1904.

_____. *An Autobiography of Buffalo Bill*. New York: Cosmopolitan Book Corp., 1920.

_____. "The Great West That Was: Buffalo Bill's Life Story," *Hearst's Magazine* (August, 1916 to July, 1917).

_____. *The Life of Hon. William F. Cody, Known as Buffalo Bill, An Autobiography*. Hartford: Frank E. Bliss, 1879.

_____. *Story of the Wild West and Camp-Fire Chats*. n.p., 1888.

_____. *True Tales of the Plains*. New York: Empire Book Co., 1908; American Press Association, 1908.

Collings, Ellsworth, and Alma Miller England. *The 101 Ranch*. Norman: University of Oklahoma Press, 1938.

Cooper, Courtney Ryley. *Annie Oakley, Woman at Arms*. Duffield & Co., 1927.

_____. "The Life and Times of Buffalo Bill," *Bell Syndicate* (March 28-May 30, 1926).

_____. *Oklahoma, A Novel*. New York: Grosset & Dunlap, 1926.

Cooper, Frank C. *Stirring Lives of Buffalo Bill and Pawnee Bill*. New York: S. I. Parsons & Co., 1912.

Cooper, Tex. "I Knew Buffalo Bill," *Frontier Times*, XXXIII (Spring, 1959), 19.

Courtney, W. B. "The Prairie Prince," *Collier's Weekly* (April 14 to May 19, 1928).

Cranbrook, James. "The Guns of Annie Oakley," *Guns*, II (May, 1956), 5-17.

Crawford, Captain Jack. *The Poet Scout*. San Francisco, 1879; New York, 1886.

Croft-Cooke, Rupert, and W. S. Meadmore. *Buffalo Bill: The Legend, the Man of Action, the Showman*. London: Sidgwick and Jackson, Ltd., 1952.

Croy, Homer. *Jesse James Was My Neighbor*. New York: Duell, Sloan and Pearce, 1949.

_____. *Our Will Rogers*. New York: Duell, Sloan and Pearce, 1953.

_____. "Texas Jack," *The Westerners New York Posse Brand Book*, II (No. 2, 1955), 29.

Curtis, E. D. "Can Women Outshoot Men?" *Guns*, I (July, 1955), 14-18, 53-54.

Day, Donald. Editor. *The Autobiography of Will Rogers*. Boston: Houghton Mifflin, 1949.

Deahl, William E., Jr. "Nebraska's Unique Contribution to the Entertainment World," *Nebraska History*, XLIX (Autumn, 1968), 283-297.

De Wolff, J. H. *Pawnee Bill (Major Gordon W. Lillie) His Experience and Adventure on the Western Plains*. Pawnee Bill's Historic Wild West Company, 1902.

Dobie, J. Frank. *The Mustangs*. Boston: Little, Brown, 1952.

Dunn, Roy Sylvan. "Buffalo Bill's Bronc Fighter," *Montana*, VII (April, 1957), 2-11.

Durant, John and Alice. *Pictorial History of the American Circus*. New York: A. S. Barnes & Co., 1957.

Elbirn, William L. "Austin Bros. 3 Ring Circus and Real Wild West," *Bandwagon* (January-February, 1962), 12-17.

Elston, Allan Vaughan. *Saddle Up for Sunlight*. Philadelphia and New York: J. B. Lippincott Co., 1952. (fiction).

Erskine, Gladys Shaw, as told to, *Broncho Charlie*. London: George G. Harrap & Co., Ltd., 1935.

Fellows, Dexter W., and Andrew A. Freeman. *This Way to the Big Show*. New York: Halcyon House, 1938.

Foote, Stella Adelyne. Editor. *Letters from Buffalo Bill*. Billings, Montana: Foote Publishing Co., 1954.

Foreman, Carolyn Thomas. *Indians Abroad*. Norman: University of Oklahoma Press, 1943.

Fowler, Gene. *A Solo in Tom-Toms*. New York: Viking Press, 1946.

_____. *Timberline*. New York: Blue Ribbon Books, 1935.

Frink, Maurice. "Buffalo Bill's Last Raid on the Sioux," *Denver Post Empire Magazine*, August 26, 1957.

Gartman, Clarence. "Last Days of Buffalo Bill," *The West* (December, 1966), 40-43, 54-57.

Gillespie, A. S. "Bud," and R. H. "Bob" Burns. *Steamboat — Symbol of Wyoming Spirit*. Laramie: University of Wyoming, 1952.

Gipson, Fred. *Fabulous Empire*. Boston: Houghton Mifflin, 1946.

Gohl, E. H. "The Effect of Wild Westing," *The Quarterly Journal of the Society of American Indians*, II (July-September, 1914), 226-228.

Griffin, Charles Eldridge. *Four Years in Europe with Buffalo Bill*. Albia, Iowa: Stage Publishing Co., 1908.

Hanesworth, Robert D. *Daddy of 'Em All*. Cheyenne: Flintlock Publishing Co., 1967.

Harvey, R. M. "Some Inside Facts about Buffalo Bill's Wild West," *Bandwagon* (January-February, 1959), 13-14.

Havighurst, Walter. *Annie Oakley of the Wild West*. New York: Macmillan, 1954.

_____. *Buffalo Bill's Great Wild West Show*. New York: Random House, 1957.

Hebberd, Mary Hardgrove. "Notes on Dr. David Franklin Powell," *Wisconsin Magazine of History* (reprint; Summer, 1952), 306-309.

Henderson, Sam. "Bronco Charley Miller," *Golden West*, II (July, 1966), 20-23, 50-52.

_____. "Those Thrilling Wild West Yesteryears," *The West*, IX (October, 1968), 16-19, 60-64.

Hill, Richmond C. *A Great White Indian Chief*. Young Buffalo Wild West and Col. Fred Cummins' Far East Combined, 1912.

Hinkle, Milt. "Circuses and Contests," *Old West*, III (Fall, 1966), 24-28.

_____. "Cowboy!" *True West*, IX (October, 1961), 38-39, 62.

_____. "The Dusky Demon," *True West*, VIII (August, 1961), 30-31, 55-57.

_____. "The Kit Carson Wild West Show," *Frontier Times*, XXXVIII (May, 1964), 6-11, 57-58.

_____. "Memoirs of My Rodeo Days," *Real West*, XI (September, 1968), 35-37, 65.

_____. "Milt Blew His Show in Chicago," *Frontier Times*, XLII (February-March, 1968), 30-31, 52-54.

_____. *Old West*. Kissimmee, Fla., n.d.

_____. "A Texan Hits the Pampas," *Old West*, II (Fall, 1965), 2-11, 40-41, 44-45, 48.

_____. "The Way a Wild West Show Operated," *Frontier Times*, XLIII (March, 1969), 20-23, 50-52.

_____. "Winning or Losing," *Frontier Times*, XLII (August-September, 1968), 26-28, 48.

_____, and Mildred Elder, "Suicide Ted Elder," *True West*, XLI (June, 1969), 40-42, 72.

Holbrook, Stewart H. *Little Annie Oakley and Other Rugged People*. New York: Macmillan, 1948.

Holm, Don. "Were There Two Buffalo Bills?" *Frontier Times*, XXXIX (September, 1965), 35, 61.

Howard, Robert West, and Oren Arnold. *Rodeo*. New York: New American Library, 1961.

Hoyt, Harloe R. *Town Hall Tonight*. Englewood Cliffs, New Jersey: Prentice-Hall, 1955.

Jacques, Hal. "Ken Maynard, King of the Cowboys," *Westerner*, I (July-August, 1969), 20-21, 61-62.

Jerrard, Leigh. "Rosa Bonheur Revealed as a Painter of Westerns," *The Westerners Brand Book*, X (August, 1953), 41-42.

Johannsen, Albert. *The House of Beadle and Adams*. Norman: University of Oklahoma Press, 1950. 2 vols.; vol. III, 1962.

Jones, Gene. "Buffalo Bill's Tragic Last Days," *Real West*, IX (March, 1966), 9, 50-51.

Katigan, Madelon B. "The Fabulous 101!" *True West*, VIII (October, 1960), 6-12, 50-51.

Kay, Jay F. "Man of Destiny," *Golden West*, I (November, 1964), 37-39, 62-64.

Kelley, Francis Beverly. "The Land of Sawdust and Spangles," *National Geographic*, LX (October, 1931), 463-516.

King, Karl L. "On the Warpath," (1915); "Passing of the Red Man," (1916); marches for band. C. L. Barnhouse, Oskaloosa, Iowa.

Kinney, Griffith. "The Haunted Corral," *Old West*, I (Fall, 1964), 2-9, 60-67.

Knight, Albert. *Wild West Waltz* (Dedicated to Miss Annie Oakley) London, n.d.

Koford, William. "Old Time Billing Wars," *Bandwagon* (May-June, 1958), 7.

Leithead, J. Edward. "Buffalo Bill Novels in Paperback Book Format," *Dime Novel Roundup*, XVII (June, 1949), 49-53.

_____. "The Wild West Shows Pass in Grand Review," *Dime Novel Roundup* (September to November, 1954).

_____. "By the Author of 'Buffalo Bill,'" *Dime Novel Roundup* (May to July, 1958).

_____. "Pulp King W. Bert Foster," *Relics*, II (Summer, 1968), 10-12.

Leonard, L. O. "Buffalo Bill's First Wild West Rehearsal," *Union Pacific Magazine* (August, 1922), 26-27.

Lillie, Gordon W. *Life Story of Pawnee Bill*. Topeka: Arthur Capper, 1916.

Mann, E. B. "Little Sure Shot," *American Rifleman*, XCVI (April, 1948), 41-44.

Mark, Frederick A. "Last of the Old West Artists — R. Farrington Elwell," *Montana*, VII (January, 1957), 58-63.

Martin's World Fair Album-Atlas and Family Souvenir, Chicago, 1892.

May, Earl Chapin. *The Circus from Rome to Ringling*. New York: Duffield & Green, 1932.

McCoy, Robert B. "Guns of the Wild West Show," *Guns*, V (February, 1959) 18-20, 64.

McCreight, M. I. "Buffalo Bill as I Knew Him," *True West*, IV (July-August, 1957), 25, 41-42.

McDaniel, Ruel. "Requiem for the Wild West Shows," *Frontier Times*, XXXVI (Winter, 1961), 22-23, 40.

Mendez, Al. "Annie Oakley," *Great West*, III (May, 1969), 12-17, 59-60.

Miller, Lee. "Tom Mix, Old Time Sheriff," *Real West*, I (November, 1958), 30-31, 61.

Morando, B. "Rodeo, the West's Oldest Sport," *Real West*, VII (July, 1964), 16-18, 45-47.

Moses, John, and Paul Selby. *The White City*. Chicago: Chicago World Book Company, 1893.

Muller, Dan. *My Life with Buffalo Bill*. Chicago: Reilly & Lee, 1948.

Mundis, Jerrold J. "He Took the Bull by the Horns," *American Heritage*, XIX (December, 1967), 50-55.

132

Murray, Marian. *Circus: From Rome to Ringling.* New York: Appleton-Century-Crofts, 1956.

Neihardt, John G. *Black Elk Speaks.* New York: William Morrow & Co., 1932.

Nolan, Paul T. "Captain Jack, the Poet Scout," *Real West,* VIII (January, 1965), 22-25, 44-45.

———. "The Western Hero on Stage," *Real West,* XI (October, 1968), 37-38, 56-57, 66, 74-75.

Nordin, Charles R. "Dr. W. F. Carver," *Nebraska History,* X (October-December, 1927).

O'Brien, Esse Forrester. *Circus: Cinders to Sawdust.* San Antonio: Naylor Co., 1959.

———. *The First Bulldogger.* San Antonio: Naylor Co., 1961.

Pachon, Stanley A. "William Wallace Cook," *Dime Novel Roundup,* XXV (September, 1957), 67-75.

Parker, Lew. *Odd People I Have Met.* n.p., privately printed, n.d.

Pfening, Fred D., Jr. *Col. Tim McCoy's Real Wild West and Rough Riders of the World.* Columbus: Pfening & Snyder, 1955.

Pfening, Fred, III. "William P. Hall," *Missouri Historical Review,* LXII (April, 1968), 286-313.

Porter, Russ. "Circus Passenger Cars," *Railroad Model Craftsman,* XXXVII (July, 1968), 19-29.

Posey, Jake. "With Buffalo Bill in Europe," *Bandwagon* (October, 1953), 4-6.

Pouska, Frank J. "Young Buffalo Wild West Show," *Bandwagon* (May-June, 1959) 15-16, 18; (July-August, 1960), 5-6, 19-20.

Red Fox, Chief William, and Lenore Sherman. "I Was with Buffalo Bill," *Real West,* XI (April, 1968), 26-28, 64-65.

Remington, Frederic, illustrator. "Behind the 'Wild West' Scenes," text by Julian Ralph. *Harper's Weekly,* XXXVIII (August 18, 1894), 775-776.

Reynolds, Chang. *Pioneer Circuses of the West.* Los Angeles: Westernlore Press, 1966.

Robinson, C. O. "Tom Mix Was My Boss," *Frontier Times,* XLIII (June-July, 1969), 18-20, 42-43.

Rock, Allen Leonard. "The Days of 'Pawnee Bill,'" *The Westerners New York Posse Brand Book,* V (No. 1, 1958).

Rosa, Joseph G. *They Called Him Wild Bill.* Norman: University of Oklahoma Press, 1964.

Roth, Charles B. "The Biggest Blow Since Galveston," *Denver Westerners Monthly Roundup,* XII (January, 1956), 4-15.

Russell, Don. "Buffalo Bill in Bound Book Fiction," *Dime Novel Roundup,* XXVII (May, 1959), 40-41.

———. *The Lives and Legends of Buffalo Bill.* Norman: University of Oklahoma Press, 1960.

———. "The Wild West and Buffalo Bill," *Facts,* III (August, 1943), 115-124.

———. Editor. "Julia Cody Goodman's Memoirs of Buffalo Bill," *Kansas State Historical Quarterly,* XXVIII (Winter, 1962), 442-496.

Sabin, Edwin L. *Buffalo Bill and the Overland Trail.* Philadelphia and London: J. B. Lippincott Co., 1914. (fiction).

Salsbury, Nate. "The Origin of the Wild West Show," "Wild West at Windsor," "At the Vatican," *Colorado,* XXXII (July, 1955), 204-215.

Savage, G. L. "Pawnee Bill, 'Little Giant of Oklahoma,'" *Old West,* III (Fall, 1966), 54-56.

Savitt, Sam. *Midnight, Champion Bucking Horse.* New York: Scholastic Book Services, 1966.

Secrest, William B. "Bill Hickok's Girl on the Flying Trapeze," *Old West,* IV (Winter, 1967), 26-30, 68.

———. "'Indian' John Nelson," *Old West,* V (Spring, 1969), 24-27, 60-63.

Sell, Henry Blackman, and Victor Weybright. *Buffalo Bill and the Wild West.* New York: Oxford University Press, 1955.

———. "Buffalo Bill and the Real Wild West," *Town and Country,* CIX (September, 1955), 80-81, 115-116.

———. "Buffalo Bill in London," *Town and Country,* CIX (October, 1955), 110-115, 149, 153-154, 156.

Shackleford, William Yancey. *Buffalo Bill Cody, Scout and Showman.* Girard, Kansas: Haldeman-Julius, 1944.

Shirley, Glenn. "Bill Pickett," *Golden West,* I November, 1964), 10-13, 52-56.

———. *Buckskin Joe.* Lincoln: University of Nebraska Press, 1966.

———. "The First Bulldogger," *Westerner,* I (November-December, 1969) 8-11, 50-51.

———. "The Home of Pawnee Bill," *Western Horseman,* XXIX (March, 1964) 56-57, 114-115.

———. *Pawnee Bill.* Albuquerque, University of New Mexico Press, 1958.

Smith, A. Morton. "Spec-ology of the Circus," *Billboard,* July 31, 1943.

Smith, DeCost. *Indian Experiences.* Caldwell, Idaho: Caxton Printers, 1943.

Smith, Helen Reagan. "Here Comes the Stagecoach," *Oklahoma Today,* XVIII (Winter, 1967-68), 27-30.

Smith, Henry Nash. *Virgin Land.* Cambridge: Harvard University Press, 1950.

Spring, Agnes Wright. *Buffalo Bill and His Horses.* Denver, 1948, 1958.

Standing Bear, Luther. *My People the Sioux.* Boston and New York: Houghton Mifflin, 1928.

Stone, Fred. *Rolling Stone.* New York and London: Whittlesey House, 1945.

Storer, Tracy I., and Lloyd P. Tevis, Jr. *California Grizzly.* Berkeley and Los Angeles: University of California Press, 1955.

Stryker, John A. "Scout's Rest Ranch," *Union Pacific Magazine* (April, 1923) 12-13.

Swartwout, Annie Fern. *Missie.* Blanchester, Ohio: Brown Publishing Co., 1947.

Taber, Bob. "Ringling and Sells-Floto Battles," *Bandwagon.* (March-April, 1959), 13.

Thanet, Octave. "The Trans-Mississippi Exposition," *Cosmopolitan,* XXV (October, 1898), 598-614.

Thompson, William C., "The Guns of Buffalo Bill," *Guns,* II (March, 1956), 28-31, 51-54.

Thorp, (Jack) Howard, and Neil M. Clark. *Pardner of the Wind.* Caldwell, Idaho: Caxton Printers, 1945.

Thorp, Raymond W. "Doc Carver vs. Buffalo Bill," *Real West,* X (March, May, 1967), No. 52, 18-20, 72-73; No. 53, 30-34.

————. "He Challenged the Champions," *Guns*, V (June, 1959), 14-16, 46-49.

————. *Spirit Gun of the West*. Glendale, California: Arthur H. Clark Co., 1957.

————. Editor. "The Letters of Doc Carver," *Outdoor Life — Outdoor Recreation* (April to July, 1930); "Those Carver Yarns," by E. L. Stevenson (August, 1930).

Tompkins, Charles H. "Gabriel Brothers Wild West Show," *The Westerners Brand Book*, XIII, (October, 1956). 64.

Trowbridge, Laura. "The Fabulous Cowboy Race," *The West*, VIII (April, 1968) 16-17, 48-50.

Vestal, Stanley [Walter S. Campbell]. *Sitting Bull, Champion of the Sioux*. Boston: Houghton Mifflin, 1932; Norman: University of Oklahoma Press, 1957.

Virgines, George W. "Adios, Amigo," *Frontier Times*, XXXIX (August-September, 1965), 21, 60, 61.

————. "Guns of the 101 Ranch," *Guns* (November, 1964) 36-37, 50-51.

————. "The Millers' Great 101 Ranch," *Golden West*, III (September, 1967), 38-39, 60-62.

————. "Presenting Miller Bros. 101 Ranch Real Wild West Show," *The Westerners Brand Book*, XXVI, (May, 1969), 25-27.

————. *Saga of the Colt Six-shooter*. New York: Frederick Fell, Inc., 1969.

Walker, Wayne T., "Bill Pickett—Bulldogger," *Great West*, III (December, 1969) 22-25, 55-56.

Walsh, Richard J., and Milton S. Salsbury. *The Making of Buffalo Bill*. Indianapolis: Bobbs-Merrill, 1928.

Watson, Elmo Scott. "The Photographs of Sitting Bull," *The Westerners Brand Book*, VI, Chicago (August, 1949), 43, 47-48.

Webb, Harry E. "Buffalo Bill As I Knew Him," *True West*, VII (November, 1967), 34-37, 64-68.

————. "My Years with Buffalo Bill's Wild West Show," *Real West*, XIII (January, 1970) 12-14, 52-55.

Westermeier, Clifford P. *Trailing the Cowboy*. Caldwell, Idaho: Caxton Printers, 1955.

Wetmore, Helen Cody. *Last of the Great Scouts*. Chicago and Duluth: Duluth Press Publishing Co., 1899.

Wilder, Marshall P. *The People I've Smiled With*. Akron, Ohio: Werner Co., 1899.

————. *The Sunny Side of the Street*. New York and London: Funk & Wagnall's, 1905.

Wilstach, John. "Buffalo Bill's Last Stands," *Esquire*, XXI (June, 1944), 46-47, 126.

Winch, Frank. "Buffalo Bill — Frontiersman," *Ace-High* (January to September, 1929).

————. *Thrilling Lives of Buffalo Bill and Pawnee Bill*. New York: S. L. Parsons & Co., 1911.

World Championship Rodeo. n.p., Whitman Publishing Co., 1957.

Yellow Robe, Chauncey. "The Menace of the Wild West Show," *Quarterly Journal of the Society of American Indians*, II (July-September, 1914), 224-228.

Yost, Nellie Irene. *Pinnacle Jake*, as told by A. B. Snyder. Caldwell, Idaho: Caxton Printers, 1951.

Index

OTHER PUBLICATIONS OF THE AMON CARTER MUSEUM INCLUDE:

Paper Talk
Illustrated Letters of Charles M. Russell
Introduction and Commentary by Frederic G. Renner

The Artist's Environment: West Coast
Text by Frederick S. Wight

Appaloosa
The Spotted Horse in Art and History
Text by Francis Haines

Taos and Santa Fe
The Artist's Environment, 1882-1942

Frontier Guns
Commentary by John Graves

Walt Kuhn
An Imaginary History of the West
Foreword by Fred S. Bartlett

Santos
The Religious Folk Art of New Mexico
Essay by George Kubler

Peter Hurd
A Portrait Sketch from Life
Text by Paul Horgan

Standing Up Country
The Canyon Lands of Utah & Arizona
Text by C. Gregory Crampton

Todd Webb Photographs
Early Western Trails and Some Ghost Towns
Introduction by Beaumont Newhall

Quiet Triumph
Forty Years with the Indian Arts Fund, Santa Fe

Brett Weston Photographs
Introduction by Nancy Newhall

Georgia O'Keffe
The Work of the Artist from 1915 to 1966
Commentaries by her contemporaries

Camposantos
A Photographic Essay by Dorothy Benrimo
Commentary by Rebecca Salsbury James and
Historical Notes by E. Boyd

T. H. O'Sullivan, Photographer
Text by Beaumont and Nancy Newhall
Published in collaboration with George Eastman House

Texas Homes of the 19th Century
Photographs by Todd Webb
Text by Drury Blakeley Alexander

Charles M. Russell
Paintings, Drawings, and Sculpture in
the Amon G. Carter Collection
A descriptive catalogue by Frederic G. Renner

Aunt Clara
The Paintings of Clara McDonald Williamson
Text by Donald and Margaret Vogel

Painting in Texas the Nineteenth Century
Text by Pauline A. Pinckney
Introduction by Jerry Bywaters

Dorothea Lange Looks At the American Country Woman
A Photographic Essay by Dorothea Lange
Commentary by Beaumont Newhall

Bartlett's West
Drawing the Mexican Boundary
Text by Robert V. Hine

Custer's Last
or The Battle of the Little Big Horn
Text by Don Russell

The Track Going Back
A Century of Transcontinental Railroading, 1869-1969
Text by Everett L. DeGolyer, Jr.

Custer's List
A Checklist of Pictures Relating to the Battle of the
Little Big Horn
Edited by Don Russell

PRODUCTION AND LITHOGRAPHY: STECK-WARLICK COMPANY, AUSTIN AND DALLAS
BOOKBINDING: UNIVERSAL BOOKBINDERY, INC., SAN ANTONIO